# 2nd Level Maths

**2B**  Practice Workbook 2

© 2024 Leckie

001/01082024

10 9 8 7 6 5 4 3 2 1

The authors assert their moral rights to be identified as the authors for this work.

All rights reserved. No part of this publication may be reproduced, stored in a retrieval system, or transmitted in any form or by any means, electronic, mechanical, photocopying, recording or otherwise, without the prior written permission of the Publisher or a licence permitting restricted copying in the United Kingdom issued by the Copyright Licensing Agency Ltd., 5th Floor, Shackleton House, 4 Battle Bridge Lane, London SE1 2HX

ISBN 9780008680367

Published by
Leckie
An imprint of HarperCollins Publishers
Westerhill Road, Bishopbriggs, Glasgow, G64 2QT

T: 0844 576 8126 F: 0844 576 8131
leckiescotland@harpercollins.co.uk www.leckiescotland.co.uk

HarperCollins Publishers
Macken House, 39/40 Mayor Street Upper, Dublin 1, D01 C9W8, Ireland

Publisher: Fiona McGlade

Special thanks
Project editor: Peter Dennis
Layout: Jouve
Proofreader: Julianna Dunn

A CIP Catalogue record for this book is available from the British Library.

Acknowledgements
Images © Shutterstock.com

Whilst every effort has been made to trace the copyright holders, in cases where this has been unsuccessful, or if any have inadvertently been overlooked, the Publishers would gladly receive any information enabling them to rectify any error or omission at the first opportunity.

Printed in the UK by Martins the Printers

This book contains FSC™ certified paper and other controlled sources to ensure responsible forest management.

For more information visit: www.harpercollins.co.uk/green

# Contents

## 6 Fractions, decimal fractions and percentages — 4
- 6.1 Identifying equivalent fractions — 4
- 6.2 Calculating equivalent fractions — 6
- 6.3 Comparing and ordering fractions — 8
- 6.4 Decimal equivalents to tenths and hundredths — 10
- 6.5 Decimal equivalents to simple fractions — 12
- 6.6 Adding and subtracting fractions — 14
- 6.7 Calculating a fraction of a value — 16
- 6.8 Comparing numbers with two decimal places — 18
- 6.9 Percentage — 20
- 6.10 Converting fractions to percentages — 22
- 6.11 Percentage calculation — 24

## 7 Money — 26
- 7.1 Money problems using the four operations — 26
- 7.2 Budgeting — 28
- 7.3 Profit and loss — 30
- 7.4 Discounts — 32
- 7.5 Credit, debit and debt — 34

## 8 Time — 36
- 8.1 Reading and writing 12-h and 24-h time — 36
- 8.2 Converting units of time using fractions — 38
- 8.3 Calculating time intervals using timetables — 41
- 8.4 Measuring time — 44
- 8.5 Speed, distance and time calculations — 46
- 8.6 Time problems — 48

## 9 Measurement — 50
- 9.1 Estimating and measuring length — 50
- 9.2 Estimating and measuring mass — 52
- 9.3 Estimating and measuring capacity — 54
- 9.4 Converting metric units — 56
- 9.5 Imperial measurement — 58
- 9.6 Calculating perimeter — 60
- 9.7 Calculating the area of regular shapes — 63
- 9.8 Calculating volume — 66

## 10 Mathematics, its impact on the world, past, present and future — 68
- 10.1 Mathematical inventions and different number systems — 68

## 11 Patterns and relationships — 70
- 11.1 Exploring and extending number sequences — 70

## 12 Expressions and equations — 72
- 12.1 Solving equations using mathematical rules — 72

## 13 2D shapes and 3D objects — 74
- 13.1 Naming and sorting shapes — 74
- 13.2 Describing and drawing circles — 76
- 13.3 Constructing 3D objects — 78
- 13.4 Constructing nets — 81

## 14 Angles, symmetry and transformation — 84
- 14.1 Identifying and sorting angles — 84
- 14.2 Measuring and drawing angles — 86
- 14.3 Finding missing angles — 88
- 14.4 Locating objects using bearings — 91
- 14.5 Reading coordinates — 94
- 14.6 Line symmetry — 98
- 14.7 Symmetrical pictures and diagrams — 100
- 14.8 Reading scale maps — 103

## 15 Data handling and analysis — 106
- 15.1 Working with a range of graphs — 106
- 15.2 Using pie charts — 109
- 15.3 Creating and interpreting graphs — 112
- 15.4 Drawing conclusions from graphs — 115

## 16 Ideas of chance and uncertainty — 118
- 16.1 Investigating the possible outcome of random events — 118

## Answers
Check your answers to this workbook online: https://collins.co.uk/pages/scottish-primary-maths

# 6.1 Identifying equivalent fractions

**1** Colour the tenths bar to show the equivalent fraction.

a) one fifth

b) two fifths

c) four fifths

d) twelve twentieths

**2** Colour the hundredths bar to show the equivalent fraction.

a) one quarter

b) three quarters

c) six eighths

d) four fifths

3. Which of these can be changed into tenths? Tick the fractions that can be changed.

a) one half

b) three fifths

c) four twentieths

## ★ Challenge

Colour each bar to create pairs of equivalent fractions. You may have to use your knowledge of simplifying. The first one is done for you.

a) eight tenths — sixteen twentieths

b)

c)

d)

e)

# 6.2 Calculating equivalent fractions

**1** Use doubling to find and write in equivalent fractions to these.

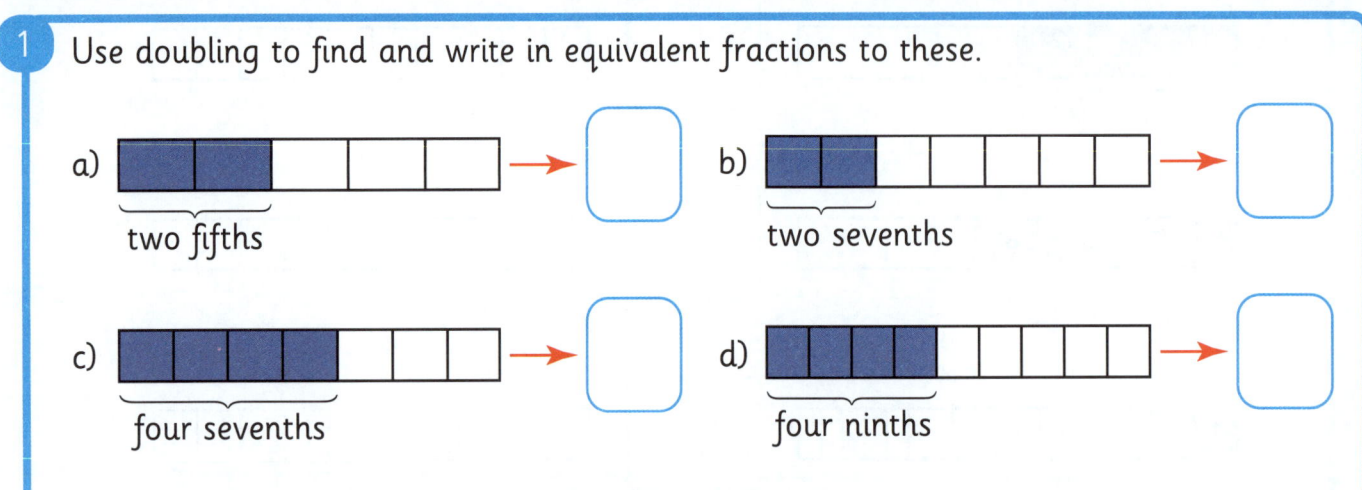

a) two fifths →

b) two sevenths →

c) four sevenths →

d) four ninths →

**2** Use multiplication to find three equivalent fractions for each of these.

a)  two fifths
- ×3 →
- ×4 →
- ×5 →

b) 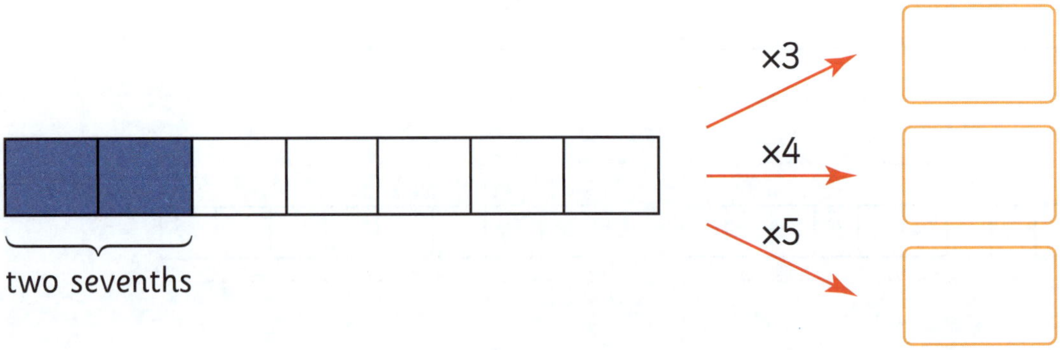 two sevenths
- ×3 →
- ×4 →
- ×5 →

c) 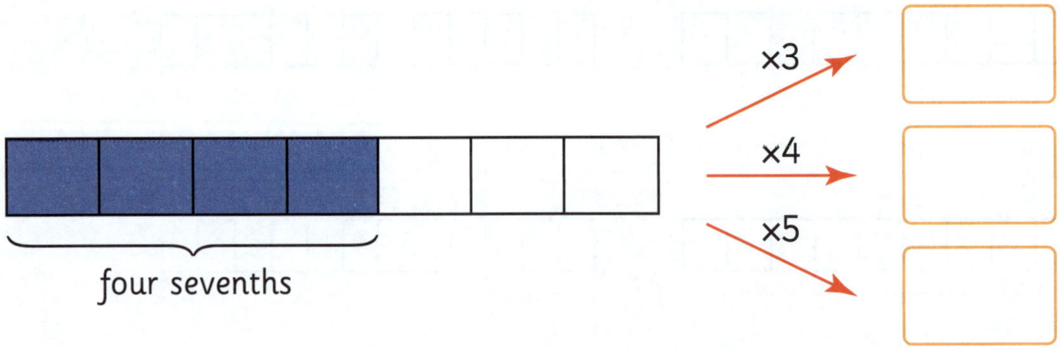 four sevenths
- ×3 →
- ×4 →
- ×5 →

d) four ninths ×3 ×4 ×5

3. Use a multiplication of your own choice to find an equivalent fraction for each of these.

a) three fifths

b) three sixths

c) five sevenths

d) five ninths

## ★ Challenge

Use these digits to make equivalent fractions. You can only use each digit once.

a) 12346   □/□ = □/□□

b) 01245   □/□ = □/□□

c) 124466  □/□ = □□/□□

# 6.3 Comparing and ordering fractions

1. Use equivalence to find which fraction is greater. Circle the greater. You can use the bars below to help you if you like.

   a) $\frac{4}{5}$ or $\frac{6}{10}$

   b) $\frac{6}{10}$ or $\frac{11}{20}$

   c) $\frac{6}{8}$ or $\frac{5}{10}$

   d) $\frac{5}{10}$ or $\frac{2}{3}$

2. Write each set of fractions in order from smallest to largest.

   a) $\frac{1}{4}$    $\frac{7}{8}$    $\frac{1}{2}$    $\frac{3}{8}$

   b) $\frac{7}{10}$    $\frac{2}{5}$    $\frac{3}{4}$    $\frac{4}{8}$

   c) $\frac{5}{6}$    $\frac{3}{4}$    $\frac{2}{3}$    $\frac{4}{5}$

3) Circle the fraction that is in the incorrect place.

a)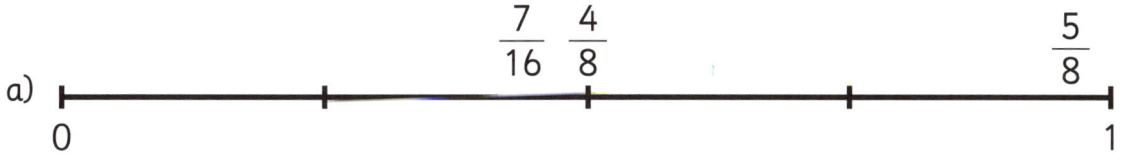

b)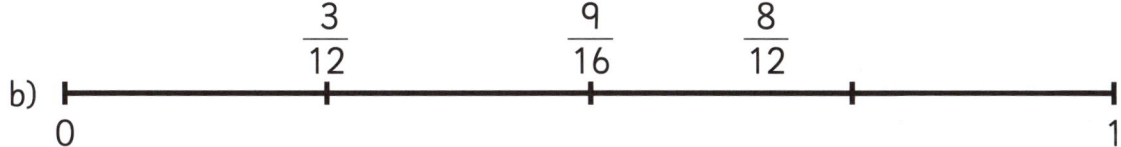

c)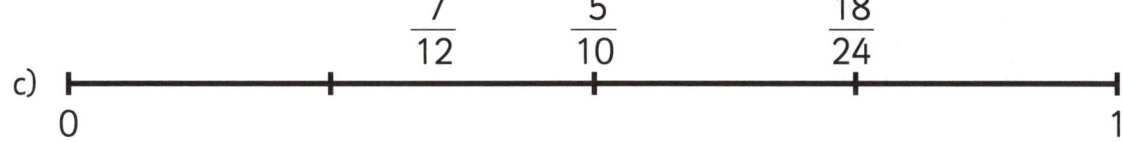

★ **Challenge**

a) Amman gets a large bar of chocolate as a present. He eats one quarter and puts the rest in the cupboard. His mum finds it and eats four sixths of what she finds. How much is left for Amman?

Draw a picture or diagram to show your thinking.

b) Finlay gets a bar of chocolate too. He eats a third. His dad finds what's left and eats two twelfths. How much is left for Finlay?

Draw a picture or diagram to show your thinking.

# 6.4 Decimal equivalents to tenths and hundredths

1) a) Mark the correct statements with a tick. The first one is done for you.

|   | Mixed fraction | Hundredths | Decimal fraction |
|---|---|---|---|
| i) | 4 wholes and 71 hundredths ✓ | 471 hundredths ✓ | 47·1 |
| ii) | 3 wholes and 91 tenths | 391 hundredths | 3·91 |

b) Write the corrections to part a) below.

i)

ii)

2) Colour the diagram to show the fraction. Write each one as a decimal fraction.

a)
45 hundredths

b)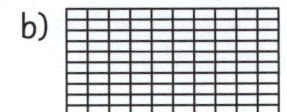
65 hundredths

c)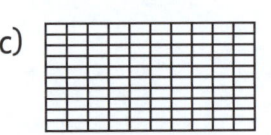
85 hundredths

d)
5 hundredths

3. Write each portion as a decimal fraction. The first one is done for you.

| | | tenths | hundredths | = | decimal fraction |
|---|---|---|---|---|---|
| a) | | 4 | 9 | | 0·49 |
| b) | | | | | |
| c) | | | | | |
| d) | | | | | |

## ★ Challenge

Each child has £1 in pennies.

$\frac{3}{6}$   $\frac{2}{5}$   $\frac{6}{8}$   $\frac{4}{6}$

Tick the children who can take exactly their fraction of £1 in pennies?

Explain your thinking here and show how many pennies each child gets.

# 6.5 Decimal equivalents to simple fractions

**1** Colour the bars to show tenths. Record the equivalent decimal fraction in the answer box. One has been done for you.

a) 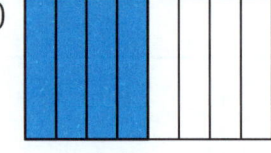 = 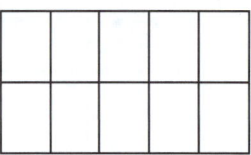 = 0·6

  three fifths    six tenths

b) 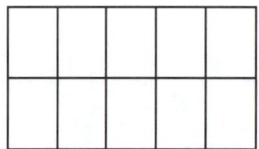 =  =

  four eighths

c) = =

  two fifths

d)  = 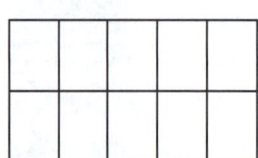 =

  six twentieths

**2** Use the boxes to help you change each fraction into a decimal fraction. Write each one as a decimal fraction. The first is done for you.

a) $\frac{3}{5}$ = 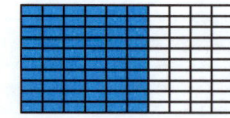 = $\frac{6}{10}$ = = 0·6

b) $\frac{3}{4}$ = = $\frac{\square}{100}$ = 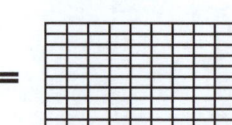 = $\square$

c) $\frac{1}{4}$ = 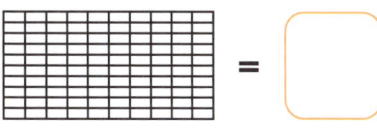 = $\frac{\square}{100}$ = ▭ = ▢

d) $\frac{50}{100}$ = ▭ = $\frac{\square}{100}$ = ▭ = ▢

**3** Match each fraction to the equivalent decimal fraction. Use the bars to help.

$\frac{9}{15}$  $\frac{12}{20}$  $\frac{6}{15}$  $\frac{8}{20}$

0·6  0·4

## ★ Challenge

Convert these to decimal fractions. Which of them is the odd one out and why? You may wish to draw or make jottings.

$\frac{16}{20}$   $\frac{40}{50}$   $\frac{15}{30}$   $\frac{20}{25}$

# 6.6 Adding and subtracting fractions

**1** Solve the following:

a) $\frac{2}{4} + \frac{1}{4} = \boxed{\phantom{0}}$

b) $\frac{5}{6} - \frac{2}{6} = \boxed{\phantom{0}}$

c) $\frac{4}{3} + \frac{1}{3} = \boxed{\phantom{0}}$

d) $\frac{5}{2} - \frac{2}{2} = \boxed{\phantom{0}}$

**2** Solve the following. Use the bar model to help you.

a) $\frac{3}{12} + \frac{4}{12} = \boxed{\phantom{0}}$

b) $\frac{7}{12} - \frac{4}{12} = \boxed{\phantom{0}}$

c) $\frac{3}{12} + \frac{8}{12} =$ ☐

d) $\frac{12}{12} - \frac{3}{12} =$ ☐

e) $\frac{15}{12} - \frac{12}{12} =$ ☐

**3** Answer the questions. You may want to use the bar models to help you.

a) Amman cuts his apple into sixths and eats four sixths. What fraction of his apple will he have left?

b) Isla and Nuria are given a bar of chocolate each. They both eat $\frac{3}{6}$ of their chocolate. How much chocolate is eaten altogether?

c) Finlay's mum cuts his birthday cake into tenths. Finlay eats $\frac{2}{10}$ and his sister eats $\frac{1}{5}$. How much cake is left?

## ★ Challenge

Use equivalence to solve these. You may want to draw bar models to help you:

a) $\frac{2}{5} + \frac{2}{10} =$

b) $\frac{6}{8} - \frac{3}{4} =$

# 6.7 Calculating a fraction of a value

1. Draw a line to match the bar model to the correct calculation and then calculate the answer.

   a) $\frac{3}{10}$ of 1320 = ☐     | 440 | 440 | 440 |

   b) $\frac{3}{5}$ of 1320 = ☐     | 220 | 220 | 220 | 220 | 220 | 220 |

   c) $\frac{3}{6}$ of 1320 = ☐     | 264 | 264 | 264 | 264 | 264 |

   d) $\frac{2}{3}$ of 1320 = ☐     | 132 | 132 | 132 | 132 | 132 | 132 | 132 | 132 | 132 | 132 |

2. Use the bar models to work out the following. The first one is done for you.

   a) | 40 | 40 | 40 | 40 |

   $\frac{3}{4}$ of 160 = 120

   b) (bar model with 8 empty cells)

   $\frac{6}{8}$ of 160 = ☐

   c) (bar model with 8 empty cells)

   $\frac{4}{8}$ of 1600 = ☐

16

**3** Draw a bar model to solve these.

a) Mr Cook bakes 736 cupcakes. He gives $\frac{5}{8}$ to his local school fair. How many does he have left?

b) Ms Shepherd looks after 2624 sheep. She sold $\frac{1}{4}$ of them at market. How many did she sell?

c) Mrs Fisher needs 2500 grams of fish to make a large fish pie. The fishmonger has $\frac{3}{5}$ of the amount she needs. How much more does she need?

★ **Challenge**

Four sports clubs share the following information about their members:

Club A has 1240 female members.
Club B has 1116 female members.
Club C has 584 female members.
Club D has 1065 female members.

Use the bar models below to calculate how many members there are in **total** at each club.

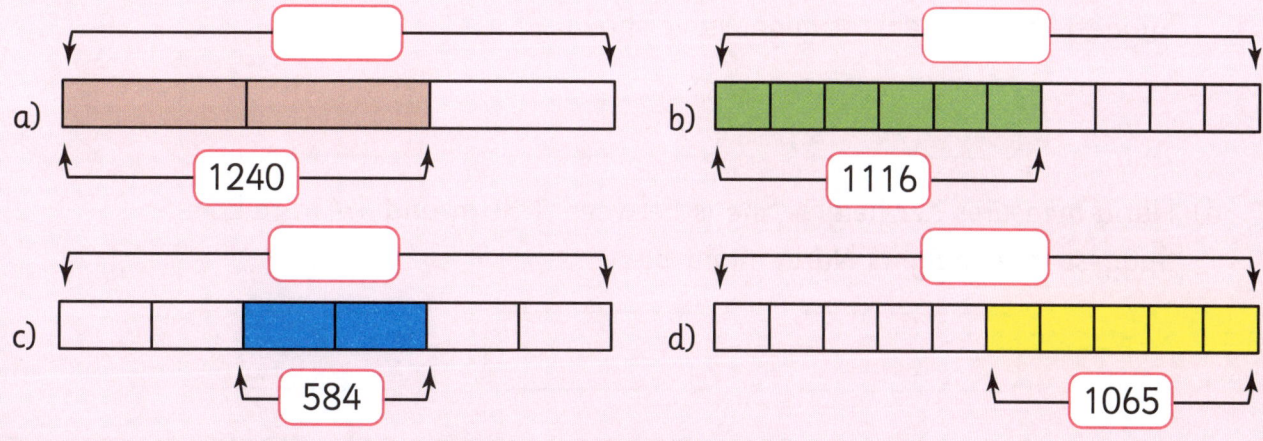

# 6.8 Comparing numbers with two decimal places

**1** Write the correct symbol **<, >** or **=** to make these statements true.

a) 0·5 ☐ 0·45  b) 0·5 ☐ 0·50  c) 1·5 ☐ 1·05

d) 2·5 ☐ 1·55  e) 2·1 ☐ 2·55  f) 2·14 ☐ 21·1

**2** Put each set of decimal numbers in order from smallest to largest.

a) 4·14   4·4   4·04   ☐ ☐ ☐

b) 14·34   14·14   14·4   ☐ ☐ ☐

c) 414·03   414·3   414·33   ☐ ☐ ☐

**3** a) Amman is saving for a new cricket bat. It costs between £79·50 and £80. Suggest three amounts it might cost.

☐ ☐ ☐

b) Isla gets a personal best for her 25 m swimming race. Her speed is between 28·45 seconds and 28·88 seconds. Suggest three times she might have recorded.

☐ ☐ ☐

c) Finlay weighs himself. The scale shows between 32·4 kg and 32·45 kg. Suggest three weights it might have shown.

☐ ☐ ☐

d) Nuria measures her height. She is between 1·36 m and 1·4 m tall. Suggest three heights Nuria might be.

☐ ☐ ☐

## Challenge

Complete the grid using these numbers.

2·05   3̶·7̶5̶   3·99   0·48   1̶·3̶5̶   0̶·1̶4̶

3·7   2·3   4̶·0̶2̶   1·3   0·36   4·6

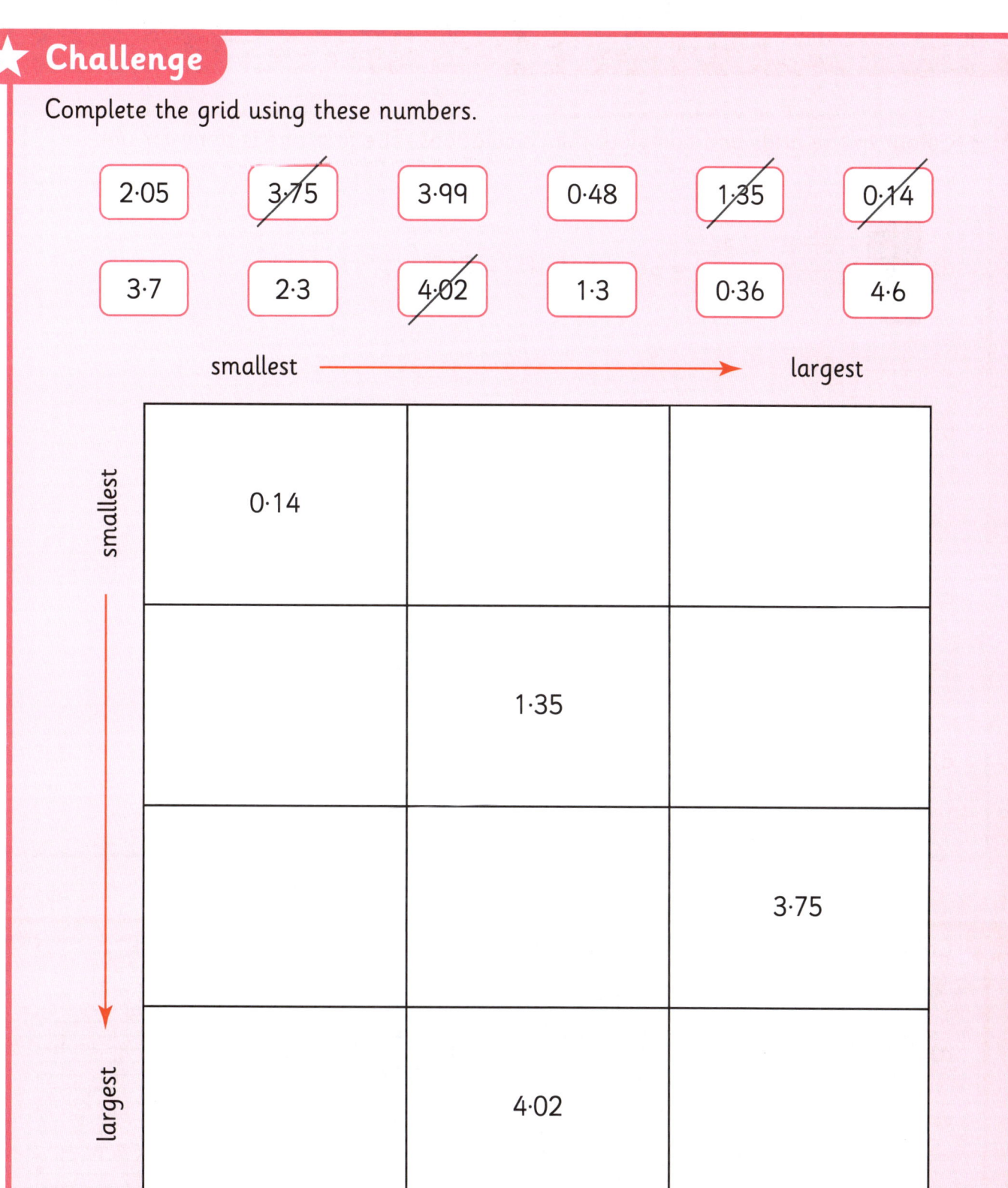

# 6.9 Percentage

**1** Colour in the grids and complete the calculations. The first one is done for you.

a) = $\dfrac{36}{100}$ = 36 out of 100 = 36%

b) = $\dfrac{46}{100}$ = ☐ out of 100 = ☐ %

c) = $\dfrac{☐}{100}$ = 56 out of 100 = ☐ %

d) = $\dfrac{☐}{100}$ = ☐ out of ☐ = 66%

**2** Colour the 100 blocks to show the following:

a) $\dfrac{45}{100}$ blue, 55% red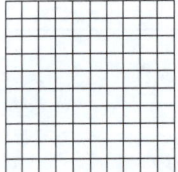

b) $\dfrac{35}{100}$ blue, 65% red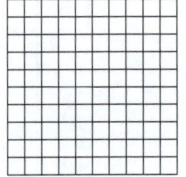

c) $\dfrac{65}{100}$ blue, 35% red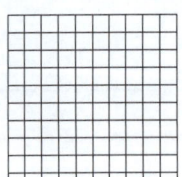

d) $\dfrac{75}{100}$ blue, 25% red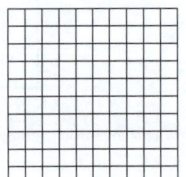

**3** Complete the following calculations. The first one has been done for you.

a) 5% = 5 out of 100 = $\frac{5}{100}$

b) 10% = ☐ out of 100 = ☐

c) 15% = ☐ out of 100 = ☐

d) 20% = ☐ out of 100 = ☐

e) 25% = ☐ out of 100 = ☐

### ★ Challenge

a) Sort the fractions into those that can have an equivalence with hundredths and those that cannot. Write your answers in the table below and you can use the grids to help you.

$\frac{8}{20}$   $\frac{9}{10}$   $\frac{8}{50}$   $\frac{8}{40}$   $\frac{9}{60}$   $\frac{8}{30}$   $\frac{9}{40}$

| Has 100 equivalent | Does not have 100 equivalent |
|---|---|
|  |  |

b) Add a fraction of your own to each side of the table.

# 6.10 Converting fractions to percentages

**1** Colour the grids and complete the following:

a) $\frac{1}{2}$ =  = $\frac{\square}{100}$

b) $\frac{1}{4}$ =  = $\frac{\square}{100}$

c) $\frac{1}{5}$ =  = $\frac{\square}{100}$

d) $\frac{2}{5}$ =  = $\frac{\square}{100}$

**2** The children have been looking at pupil data in their school.

a) 50% of the P7 class walk to school. What % do not walk to school? ☐

b) 55% of the twins in school are non-identical. What % are identical? ☐

c) 5% of the pupils in P6 are left-handed. What % are right-handed? ☐

d) 25% of P5 pupils speak more than one language. What % speak only one language? ☐

3. Use these numbers to create six different fractions and convert them to percentages. One has been done for you.

**Numerator**   4  or  8

**Denominator**   10  or  20  or  50

a) $\dfrac{4}{10} = \dfrac{40}{100} = 40\%$

b) $\dfrac{\square}{\square} = \dfrac{\square}{100} = \square \%$

c) $\dfrac{\square}{\square} = \dfrac{\square}{100} = \square \%$

d) $\dfrac{\square}{\square} = \dfrac{\square}{100} = \square \%$

e) $\dfrac{\square}{\square} = \dfrac{\square}{100} = \square \%$

f) $\dfrac{\square}{\square} = \dfrac{\square}{100} = \square \%$

★ **Challenge**

Nuria says that you can tell if a fraction can convert to a percentage if you know the denominator. Isla says you need to know the numerator **and** the denominator.
Show some examples to prove who is correct and why.

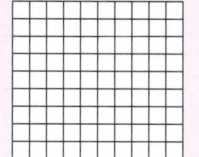 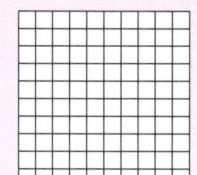 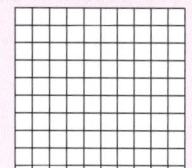 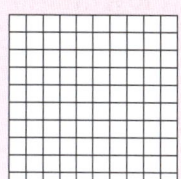

# 6.11 Percentage calculation

1. Use the bar models to calculate the percentage of children for each school who walk to school or travel by car.

**Glenfield School – 100 children**

a)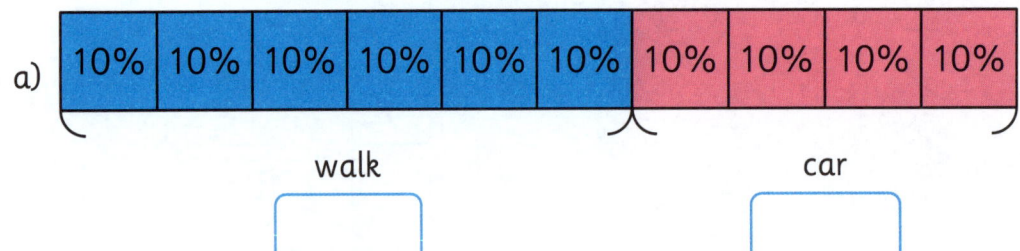

walk ☐   car ☐

**Seaview School – 90 children**

b)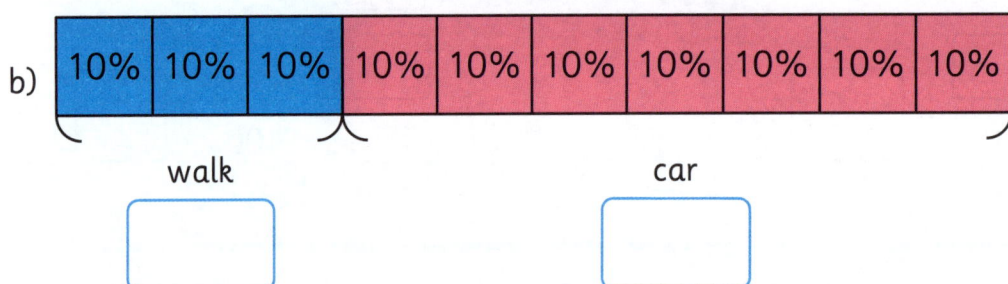

walk ☐   car ☐

2. Draw a bar model to solve each of these.

   a) Amman hands a bag of 10 books into the charity shop. 60% of them are picture books. How many are not picture books?

   b) Nuria's parents invite 80 people to a party. 20% reply to say they cannot make it. How many guests can Nuria's parents expect?

**3** Fieldview School has 120 pupils.

a) At lunch time, 10% of children go home. How many children go home?

b) At lunch time, 30% of children have a vegetarian school dinner. How many children have a vegetarian dinner?

c) At lunch time, 40% of children have a non-vegetarian school dinner. How many children have a non-vegetarian dinner?

d) At lunch time, the rest of the children have a packed lunch. How many children have a packed lunch?

What percentage of the school is this?

## ★ Challenge

The children are having a netball competition. Who has the most success? Explain your answer.

Amman tries 30 times and gets 15 balls in the net.

Nuria tries 25 times and gets 12 balls in the net.

Finlay tries 40 times and gets 24 balls in the net.

Isla tries 20 times and gets 14 balls in the net.

# 7.1 Money problems using the four operations

**1** Complete the table. The first is done for you.

| Amount | Pounds and pence | Pence |
|---|---|---|
| Three pounds sixty | £3·60 | 360p |
| Three pounds six | | |
| | £4·08 | |
| | | 480p |
| Fourteen pounds ten | | |
| | £24·20 | |

**2** Answer the following questions. You may prefer to convert the amounts to pence to work out the calculations. Give your answers in pounds and pence.

a) i) The hairdresser charges £22 for Nuria to have her hair cut. Nuria also buys a bottle of shampoo for £3·45 and pays the hairdresser. How much does she pay in total?

ii) Nuria gets £14·55 in change. How much did she give the hairdresser?

iii) What notes might she have paid with? Show three ways.

| | | |
|---|---|---|
| | | |

b) Nuria and her mum go to a café after the hair cut. They both have a milkshake and buy a fudge brownie to share.

**Menu**

| | |
|---|---|
| Milkshake | £2 |
| Fudge Brownie | £4·50 |
| Scone | £1·79 |

Mum pays with a note and three coins. What note and coins did she use?

## ★ Challenge

The four children do a sponsored 10 km walk.

- Nuria gets £2·25 for each kilometre.
- Amman gets £3·05 for each kilometre.
- Finlay gets £4·35 for each kilometre.
- Isla gets £2·45 for each kilometre.

a) How much does each child make?

b) How much do the children make altogether?

# 7.2 Budgeting

**1** Nuria is shopping for dog treats. She wants to get the best deal. Circle the best deal for each item and explain your thinking.

| Item | Molly's Market | Patrick's Pets | Reason |
|---|---|---|---|
| a) Chew Bones | 10 for £3·99 | 20 for £7·50 | |
| b) Doggie Drops | Pack of 100 for £6·50 | Pack of 10 for 70p | |
| c) Pet Dental Sticks | Pack of 20 for £1·99 | Pack of 40 for £3·00 | |

**2** Solve the following:

a) A cinema ticket is £6·00. A medium bag of popcorn is £5·00. A monthly ticket is £25 and includes one free bag of popcorn and free entry to the cinema four times. Isla knows she wants to go to three films in January and she likes a bag of popcorn each time. Should she get the monthly ticket or not?
Explain your thinking.

b) Cornflakes come in two sizes at the supermarket: a 1 kg box for £1·20 or a 500 g box for 70p. How much will Nuria save if she buys the best deal?

c) Dad is buying cupcakes for Amman's birthday party. He needs 30 cupcakes. A local baker will bake them for £1·12 each. She will put Amman's name on each and decorate them in Amman's favourite colour. The supermarket has packs of six cupcakes for £6·60. Who should Dad buy the cupcakes from and why?

### ★ Challenge

Some of Finlay's family are going on holiday. There is one adult and three children.

**Zippy Holidays**

Return flights: £180 per adult
£120 per child

Hotel: £600 for family room

Breakfast: £160 for the stay

**Flying Fox Holidays**

Return flights: £500 for 4 people

Hotel: £850 for family room (includes Breakfast)

a) Which deal offers the best value for Finlay's family?

b) If the family buys the best deal and saves £100 each month, how long will it take them to have enough money to pay for the holiday?

# 7.3 Profit and loss

1) Decide whether the sale gives a profit or a loss.

| Item | Bought | Sold | Profit or loss? |
|---|---|---|---|
| Car | £28 490 | £18 000 | |
| House | £399 405 | £410 245 | |
| Mobile phone | £449·00 | £350·00 | |
| Concert ticket | £105·00 | £120·00 | |

2) The school tuck shop buys a box of 32 crisps for £19. The staff sell the packets of crisps for 70p each.

a) Does the school make a profit or a loss?

b) How much did they make or lose?

3) Mrs Logan buys a new coat for £77 in January. In July she sells it for £55.

a) Did she make a profit or a loss?

b) How much did she make or lose?

**4** Mr Good and Mr Sharp buy a flat. They pay £62 000. They spend £2400 on repairs. They sell the flat a year later for £82 000.

a) Did they make a profit or a loss?

b) How much did they make or lose?

## ★ Challenge

Isla and Nuria are raising money for charity and are planning a disco. They have set themselves a target of raising £400.

- They get some decorations for free.
- They pay £50 to hire the hall from 6 pm–10 pm.
- The disco costs £275 for 4 hours.

a) How much do the children need to raise to make a profit?

b) How much do the children need to raise to meet their charity target?

c) If 100 children buy a ticket, how much must the ticket cost so that the children make their target?

# 7.4 Discounts

**1** Work out the new price for each of these items.

| Item | Cost | Discount | New cost |
|---|---|---|---|
|  | £3·80 | 50% off |  |
|  | £1·20 | Half price |  |
|  | £2·00 | 10% off |  |
|  | £1·60 | 25% off |  |

a) Mr Bigg has a sale in his shop. He puts a big sign in the window: 10% off all goods. How much does each item cost now?

b) Mrs Bigg thinks the sale should be better. She takes down the 10% off sign and puts a 25% off sign up.

How much does each item cost now?

3. In the sale, Amman pays £3·05 for a cap which is half price. How much did the cap cost originally?

### Challenge

a) There is a sale at the toy shop. Nuria wants a video game which has 25% off and is now £18. What was the original price? Show your working.

b) Finlay wants a board game which has 75% off and is now £9. What was the original price? Show your working.

# 7.5 Credit, debit and debt

**1** Look at Mrs Smith's bank statement and complete the balance column.

| | (£) In | (£) Out | (£) Balance |
|---|---|---|---|
| | | | 3500 |
| Café | | 22·00 | 3478 |
| Petrol | | 88·00 | 3390 |
| Gas | | 216·00 | 3174 |
| Shopping | | 125·00 | 3049 |
| Pay | 600·00 | | 3649 |
| Council tax | | 350·00 | 3299 |

Is she in debt or in credit at the end? **in credit**

**2** Look at Mr Smith's bank statement and complete the balance column.

| | (£) In | (£) Out | (£) Balance |
|---|---|---|---|
| | | | 500 |
| Petrol | | 40·00 | 460 |
| Birthday | 50·00 | | 510 |
| Shopping | | 122·00 | 388 |
| Energy | | 215·00 | 173 |
| Clothes | | 60·00 | 113 |
| Car | | 152·00 | −39 |
| Dog food | | 27·00 | −66 |

Is he in debt or in credit at the end? **in debt**

**3** Look at the information for Mr Ahmed's credit card account.

**Credit limit £2000**

| | |
|---|---|
| Flights | £600·00 |
| Concert tickets | £120·00 |
| PAYMENT – THANK YOU | £900·00 CR |
| Train | £125·00 |
| Restaurant | £97·00 |
| Petrol station | £77·00 |
| Cinema | £34·00 |
| Present balance | |
| Available to spend | |

Calculate Mr Ahmed's balance and how much he has to spend. CR means that a payment has been made.

## ★ Challenge

You can borrow £400 with your credit card. Think of something you would like to buy.

What is the item and the cost?

a) If you do not pay your credit card in time, you will have to pay an extra 10% of the amount you owe. How much is this?

b) Explain a different way to pay for your item.

# 8.1 Reading and writing 12-h and 24-h time

**1** Complete these:

a) 1 + 12 = ☐

b) 11 + 12 = ☐

c) ☐ + 12 = 22

d) ☐ + 12 = 21

e) 8 + ☐ = 20

f) 7 + ☐ = 19

g) ☐ + 12 = 17

h) ☐ + 12 = 18

**2** Fill in the missing equivalent times:

| 12-hour clock | 24-hour clock |
|---|---|
| 2·00 pm | 1400 |
| 2·30 pm | |
| 2·45 pm | |
| 3·45 pm | |
| 4·30 pm | |
| 5·30 pm | |
| 6·30 pm | |
| | 1845 |
| | 1945 |
| | 2000 |
| | 2100 |
| | 2130 |
| | 2230 |
| | 2330 |

**3** Write these times in the table below. Start with the earliest time and write them in order.

a) 0801   b) 8·01 pm   c) 2000   d) 8·00 am   e) 12·01 am
f) 0002   g) 12·03 pm   h) 1204   i) 2359   j) 1159

| Between midnight and noon | Between noon and midnight |
|---|---|
|  |  |

**4** Put the following in time order starting with the time in bold:

a) 3·00 pm   1440   1240   **11·40 am**

b) 12·50 am   **0040**   1040   10·40 pm

c) **1600**   4·15 pm   0415   4·00 am

★ **Challenge**

Amman is meeting Finlay at the park. He wrote the time on a piece of paper but he has lost it. He remembers writing down **0** twice and a **4**. He knows it was in the afternoon. He remembers using 24-hour time. What time is Amman supposed to meet Finlay?

# 8.2 Converting units of time using fractions

**1** This number line and the clock face both show 60 minutes.

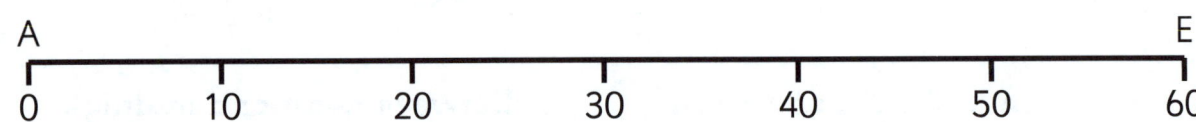

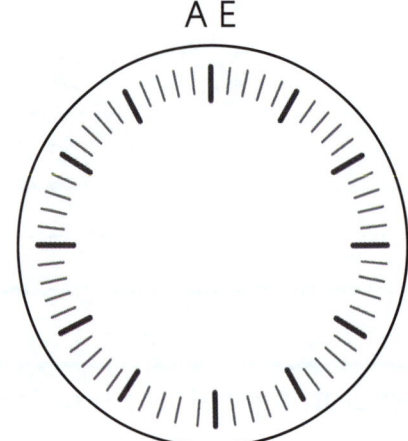

Write the following on the number line and the clock face and answer the questions.

**A** at zero minutes

**C** at the halfway point. Half of 60 = ☐

**B** halfway between **A** and **C**. One quarter of 60 = ☐

**D** halfway between C and E. Three quarters of 60 = ☐

$\frac{1}{4}$ of an hour = ☐ minutes.

$\frac{1}{2}$ an hour = ☐ minutes.

$\frac{3}{4}$ of an hour = ☐ minutes.

1 hour = ☐ minutes.

**2** Answer the following calculations:

a) 0900 + $\frac{1}{2}$ an hour =

b) 0915 + $\frac{1}{2}$ an hour =

c) 0930 + $\frac{1}{2}$ an hour =

d) 7·00 pm + $\frac{3}{4}$ of an hour =

e) 7·15 pm + $\frac{3}{4}$ of an hour =

f) 7·30 pm + $\frac{3}{4}$ of an hour =

**3** Draw the correct time on the clock faces.

a) Isla is going to meet Nuria at 2·20 pm. It takes her half an hour to walk to Nuria's house. When should she set out?

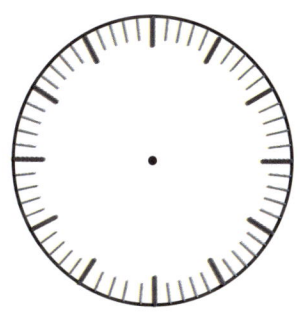

b) Finlay sets off for school at 8·25 am. He takes a quarter of an hour to get to school. When does he arrive?

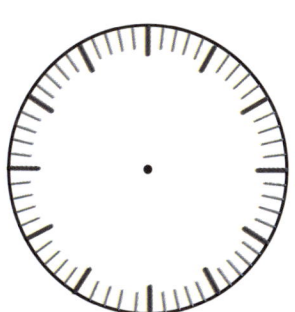

c) At school the children get three quarters of an hour for lunch. If lunch break starts at 12·40 pm, when will it end?

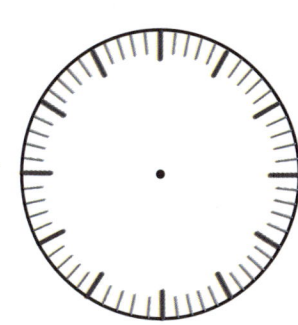

**Challenge**

You need to play this game with a partner or play as two different people! Use a dice.

$\frac{1}{4}$ hour     15 minutes     $\frac{1}{2}$ an hour     30 minutes     $\frac{3}{4}$ hour     45 minutes

Both players start at 9·00 am. Roll the dice and add the matching amount of time. For example, if you roll a 3 you add $\frac{1}{2}$ an hour. Keep a running total. The winner is the first player to reach 3 pm.

| Player 1 | Player 2 |
|---|---|
| 9·00 am | 9·00 am |
| | |
| | |
| | |
| | |
| | |
| | |
| | |
| | |
| | |
| | |
| | |
| | |

# 8.3 Calculating time intervals using timetables

**1** Use the timetable to answer the questions.

| Channel 1 | Channel 2 | Channel 3 |
|---|---|---|
| **1610** Mr Moon | **1600** Cannonball | **1700** Evening News |
| **1620** Antman | **1610** Doris | **1725** Weather |
| **1640** Beat the Teacher | **1620** Power Pets | **1730** Snooker |
| **1655** News Time | **1635** Magic Tunes | **1830** Health Hotel |
| **1705** Red Robin | **1650** Space Adventure | **1915** Who Eats What? |
| **1735** Quizzer | **1700** News and Views | **1945** Greenside |
| **1800** News | **1730** Fashion Fun | **2030** Bingo Balls |
| **1835** Scotland Latest | **1750** Cat and Carrot | **2100** New House Old House |
| **1900** Bill and Bob | **1810** Weather Report | **2200** Late News |

a) Nuria starts watching TV at 1600 and went to have tea at the end of Red Robin. How long was she watching television for?

b) Finlay watches Antman and Space Adventure. How long does he watch TV?

c) Isla watches a news programme that lasts longer than half an hour. Which channel is she watching?

d) Amman starts to watch Channel 3 at 1730. He watches TV for 90 minutes. What programme is on TV when he switches off the telly?

e) What programmes could these people be watching?

| Name | Channel | Length of programme | Name of programme |
|---|---|---|---|
| Billy | Channel 2 | 15 minutes | |
| Alisha | Channel 3 | 45 minutes | |
| Cameron | Channel 1 | 10 minutes | |

2. Here is a train timetable for trains from Edinburgh to Glasgow. Calculate the journey time for each train.

|  | A | B | C | D | E |
|---|---|---|---|---|---|
| **Edinburgh** | 1208 | 1239 | 1245 | 1312 | 1315 |
| **Glasgow** | 1330 | 1400 | 1337 | 1430 | 1406 |

Train A:   Train B:   Train C:   Train D:   Train E:

## Challenge

a) Complete the bus timetable for the Number 72 bus route.

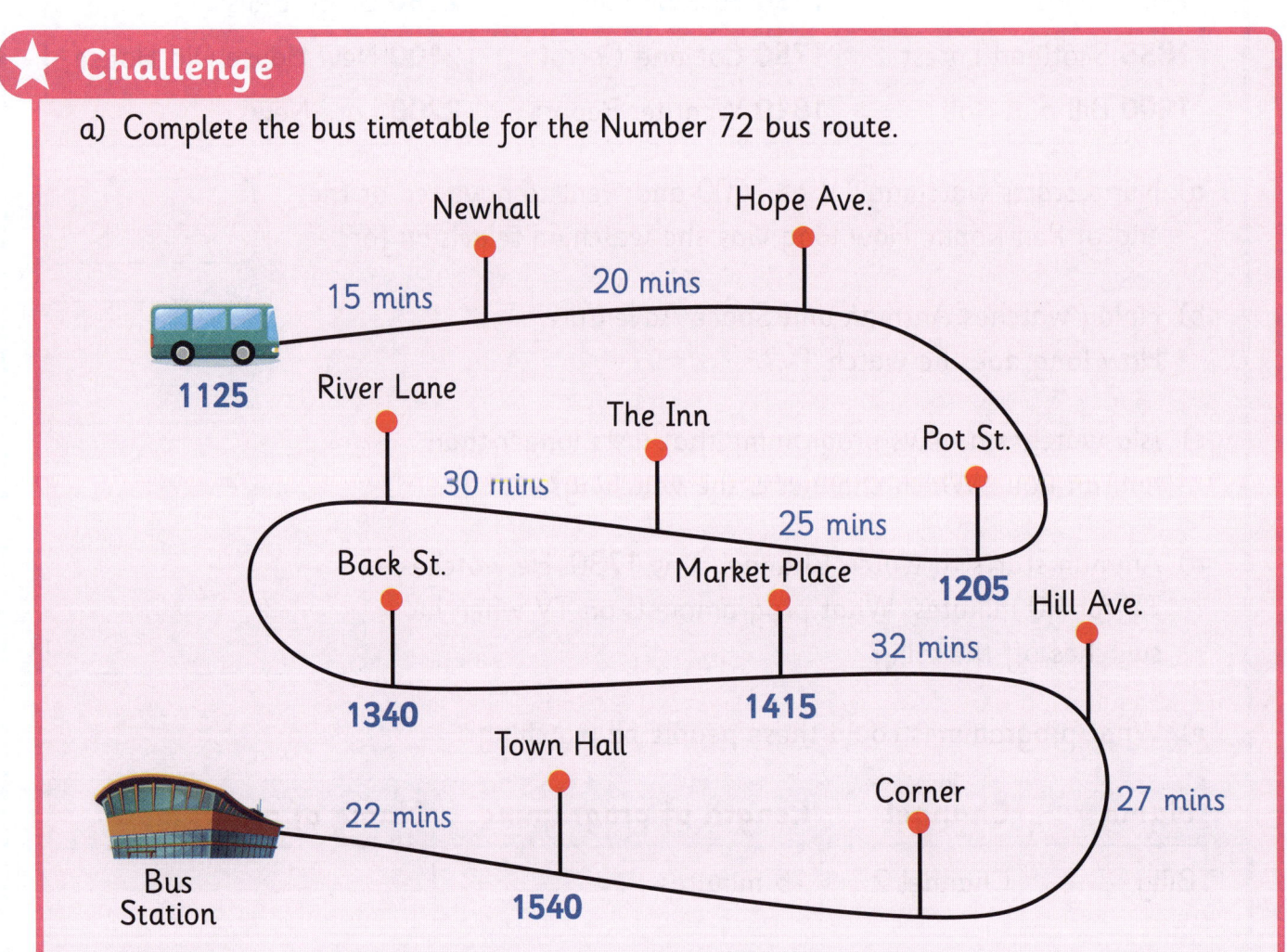

| Bus stop | Time | Length of journey (minutes) |
|---|---|---|
| Start | 1125 | |
| Newhall | 1140 | 15 |
| Hope Ave | | |
| Pot St | | |
| The Inn | | |
| River Lane | | |
| Back St | | |
| Market Place | | |
| Hill Ave | | |
| Corner | | |
| Town Hall | | |
| Bus Station | | |

b) Draw your own bus map and timetable. Use a separate piece of paper if you need to.

## 8.4 Measuring time

**1** Which unit would be best for measuring time in these situations. Tick the correct box.

|  | seconds | minutes | hours | days |
|---|---|---|---|---|
| Saying your name aloud |  |  |  |  |
| The Olympic Games |  |  |  |  |
| A film at the cinema |  |  |  |  |
| A song on the radio |  |  |  |  |
| Getting dressed for school |  |  |  |  |

**2** For each activity estimate how long it will take you to do it, then time yourself. Record your estimate and time in the table.

|  | Estimate more or less than a minute | Actual time |
|---|---|---|
| Writing your name backwards |  |  |
| Walking to the door and back |  |  |
| Reading a page of a book |  |  |
| Putting your jacket on |  |  |
| Asking five children their favourite colour |  |  |

3. Make a list of all the devices in your house and/or school that can be used to measure time.

|  |  |  |
|---|---|---|
|  |  |  |
|  |  |  |

## ⭐ Challenge

Read the list below. You are going to create a birthday card for a friend. Time how long it takes to do each part.

| Activity: Create a birthday card | Time |
|---|---|
| Getting resources together |  |
| Folding card |  |
| Drawing picture |  |
| Colouring picture |  |
| Writing message |  |

# 8.5 Speed, distance and time calculations

Can you solve these problems using what you know about the link between speed, distance and time?

1. Mr Thomson drives at 20 miles per hour (mph) for 30 minutes. How far does he travel?

2. Ms Khan drives at 60 mph for $2\frac{1}{2}$ hours. How far did she travel?

3. Mrs Lee runs for $1\frac{1}{2}$ hours at a speed of 10 mph. How far did she run?

4. Mr Choi drives at 50 mph and travels 50 miles. How long was he driving for?

5. Mrs Gray drives at 20 mph and travels 5 miles. How long was she driving for?

6. Ms Anderson cycles at 15 mph and travels 30 miles. How long was she cycling for?

## Challenge

a) Measure a distance of 10 metres and mark it. You will need a calculator. Use this to work out your speed for these:

To find the speed travelled in kilometres per hour, follow these steps:
1. Ensure your estimated time to travel 1000 m is in minutes.
2. Divide 60 (minutes) by your estimated time to travel 1000 m.

|  | Time to travel 10 metres | Time to travel 100 metres | Estimated time to travel 1000 m (1 km) | Speed travelled in kilometres per hour |
|---|---|---|---|---|
| Hopping |  |  |  |  |
| Running forwards |  |  |  |  |
| Running backwards |  |  |  |  |
| Dribbling a ball |  |  |  |  |
| Skipping |  |  |  |  |

b) Measure a distance of 20 metres and mark it. Use this to work out your speed for these:

| Activity | Time to travel 20 metres | Time to travel 100 metres | Estimated time to travel 1000 m | Speed travelled in kilometres per hour |
|---|---|---|---|---|
| Hopping |  |  |  |  |
| Running forwards |  |  |  |  |
| Running backwards |  |  |  |  |
| Dribbling a ball |  |  |  |  |
| Skipping |  |  |  |  |

# 8.6 Time problems

**1** Amman walks 25 minutes to Nuria's house and waits 15 minutes for her to get ready. They then walk 25 minutes to meet Finlay. How long was it until Amman and Finlay met up? Write your answer in hours and minutes.

**2** The four children have to look after the book sale at the school fair. The fair lasts from 10 am until 12·40 pm How long does each child have to look after the stall if they all do the same amount of time?

**3** Isla was 12 minutes late for her dance class. The class lasts an hour and a quarter. How long did Isla spend at that class? Write your answer in hours and minutes.

**4** Nuria wants to swim 200 metres in under 6 minutes. Her latest time is 340 seconds. Has she been successful? Explain your answer.

**5** Nuria and Isla go shopping on Saturday. They leave at 1430. The bus journey into town takes 10 minutes and they spend 90 minutes shopping. They go to a café for 35 minutes and then return home. What time do they return home?

**6** Amman walks to and from school twice a week. The journey one way takes him 25 minutes. How long does Amman take walking to and from school in a fortnight?

## ★ Challenge

Write the date and time now. Date: [ ]   Time: [ ]

Use the information above to answer the following:

a) In ten minutes the time will be

b) In twenty minutes the time will be

c) In 240 seconds the time will be

d) In 24 hours the date and time will be

e) In 8 days the date will be

f) In 2 months the date will be

g) In 48 days the date will be

# 9.1 Estimating and measuring length

**1** Use a ruler to draw these lines. Then write the length in centimetres.

a) 60 mm                                     ☐ cm

b) 69 mm                                     ☐ cm

**2** Fill in the distances in kilometres. Use the most direct route.

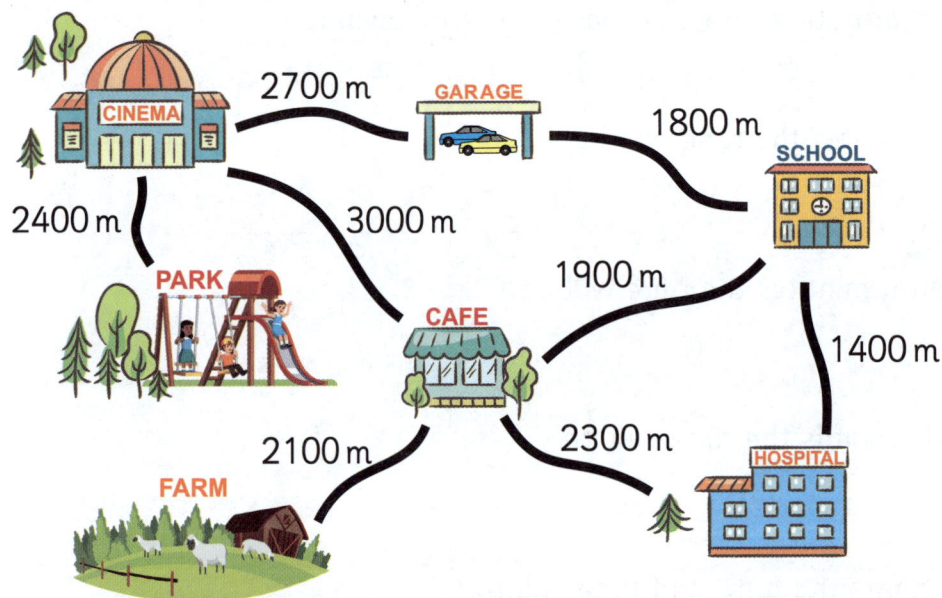

| From | To | Distance in km |
|---|---|---|
| hospital | school | |
| farm | cafe | |
| cinema | park | |
| garage | cinema | |
| garage | school | |
| cinema | hospital | |
| farm | school | |
| cafe | park | |

3. You will need a measuring tape, something to throw and your workbook. Go to a place you can throw your object. Estimate and measure a distance of 1·4 m. Throw your object and measure where it lands.

| Object | Distance where it lands in cm |
|---|---|
| First throw | |
| Second throw | |
| Third throw | |
| Fourth throw | |

## Challenge

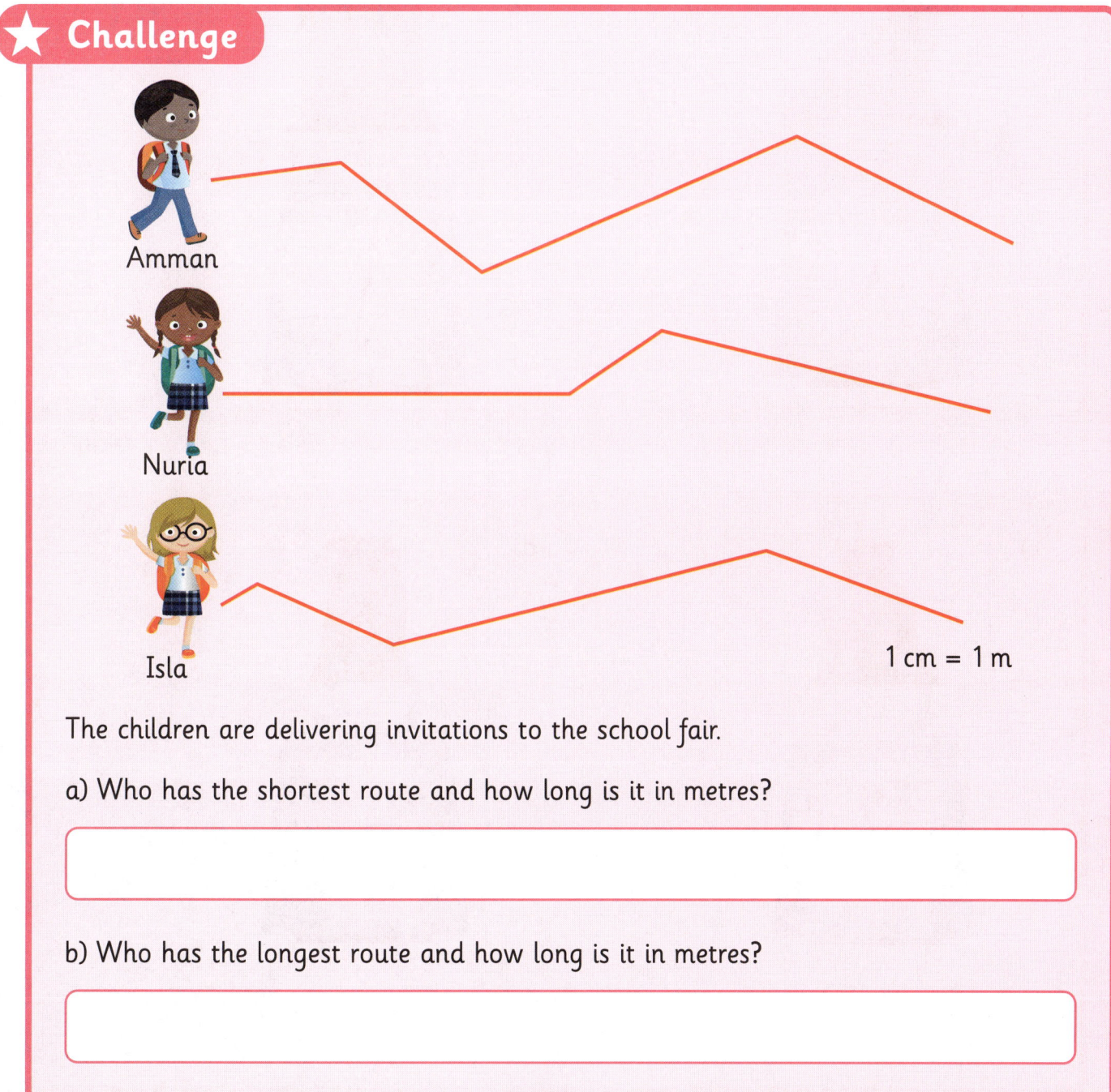

The children are delivering invitations to the school fair.

a) Who has the shortest route and how long is it in metres?

b) Who has the longest route and how long is it in metres?

# 9.2 Estimating and measuring mass

1. A kilogram can be divided into ten equal parts. Complete the diagram.

| 100 g | | | 400 g | | | | | | |
|---|---|---|---|---|---|---|---|---|---|
| 0·1 kg | | | | | | 0·7 kg | | | |

2. Write the mass of each sack in grams and kilograms.

a)

b)

c)

d)

**3** a) Find three items that you estimate to have a mass of more than 1 kg but less than 1·5 kg.

| Item | Estimated mass in kg | Actual mass in kg |
|---|---|---|
|  |  |  |
|  |  |  |
|  |  |  |

b) Put the items in order from lightest to heaviest.

⭐ **Challenge**

a) Use cardboard, paper and tape to build a bridge. It must hold 0·25 kg. Draw a diagram of your bridge.

b) Keep adding weights until your bridge collapses. How much did it manage to hold **before** it collapsed?

# 9.3 Estimating and measuring capacity

**1** Write the amount of liquid in each jug.

a) [ ] millilitres    [ ] litres

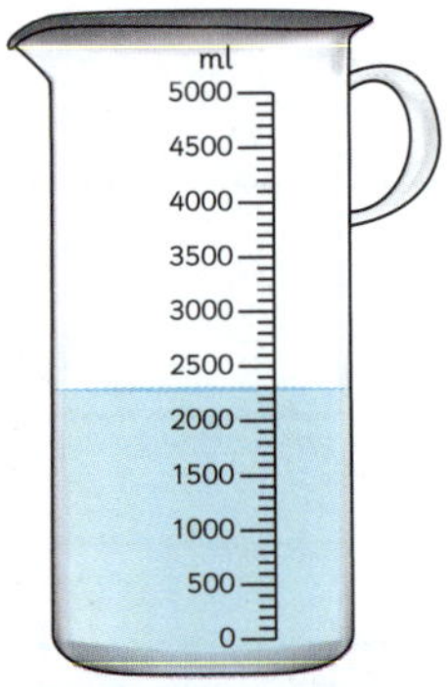

b) [ ] millilitres    [ ] litres

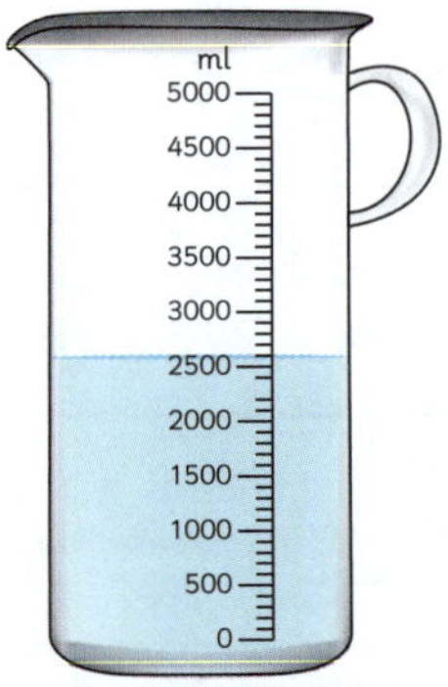

c) [ ] millilitres    [ ] litres

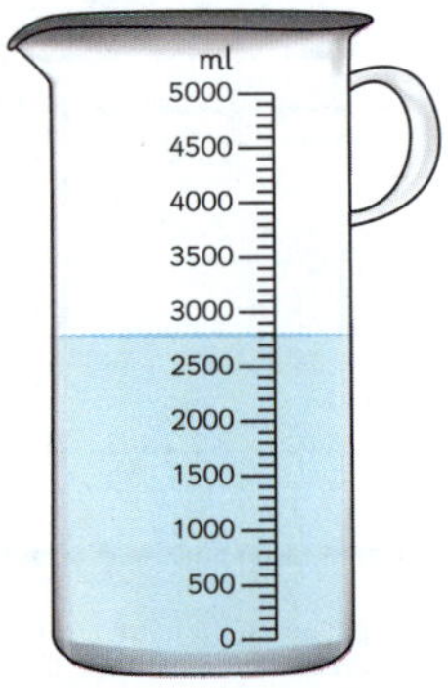

d) [ ] millilitres    [ ] litres

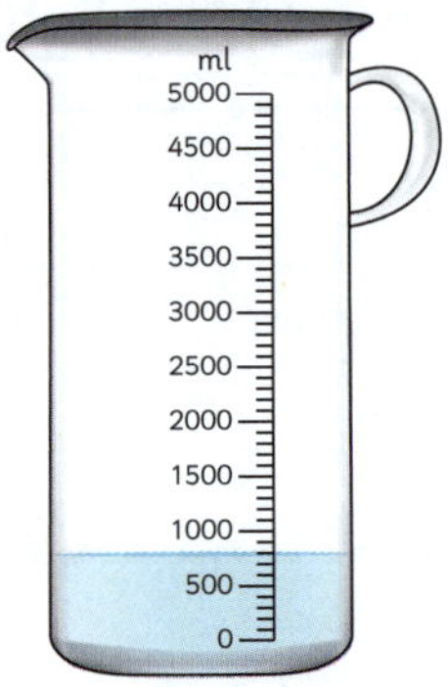

**2** Fill with the correct amount of liquid by colouring these jugs.

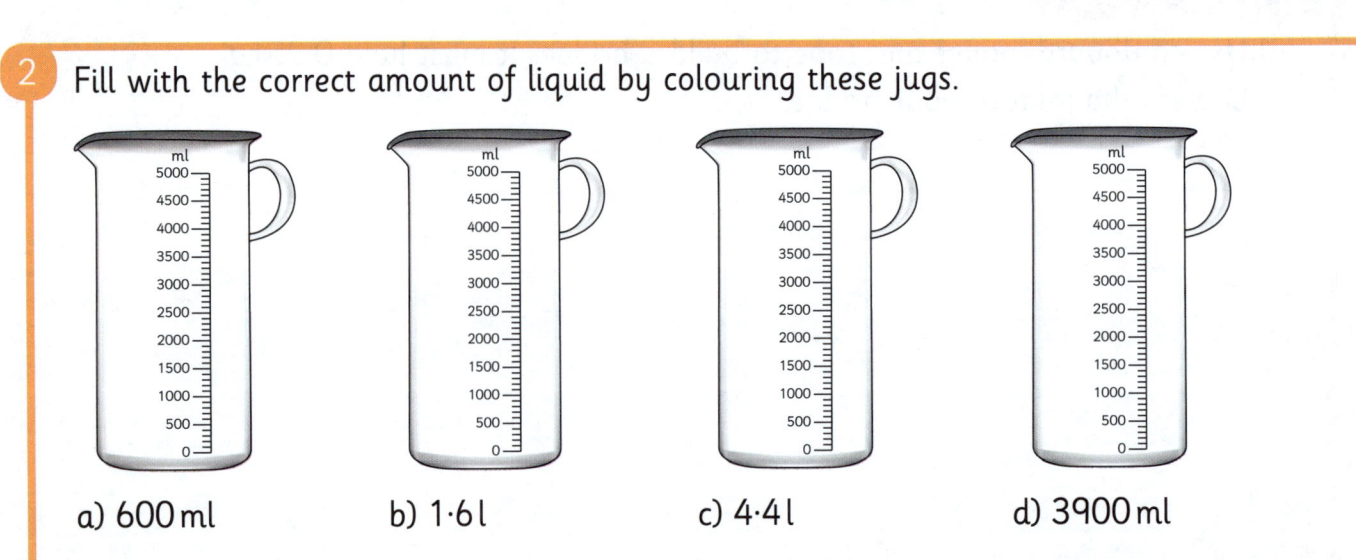

a) 600 ml    b) 1·6 l    c) 4·4 l    d) 3900 ml

3. Draw lines to match these measurements.

1·2 litres

1·2 l

12 litres

12000 ml

120 millilitres

0·120 l

1200 ml

1·20 litres

★ **Challenge**

Isla has an empty bottle that holds 4 litres of water. Finlay has an empty bottle that holds 7 litres of water. The children are at the classroom sink. Amman challenges them to bring him 5 litres using only their two bottles.

How can Isla and Finlay get 5 litres using only their bottles?

# 9.4 Converting metric units

1. Capacity measures the amount a container can hold. Volume is the space taken up by a 3D shape. Circle the items below that can have capacity.

2. Complete the table. The first one is done for you.

| Cubic centimetres | | millilitres |
|---|---|---|
| 45 cm³ | is the same as | 45 ml |
| 55 cm³ | is the same as | |
| | is the same as | 550 ml |
| 505 cm³ | is the same as | |
| | is the same as | 1 litre |

3. Imagine each of these filled with cubic centimetres. Write in the volume and capacity.

a)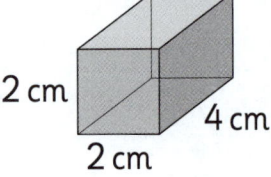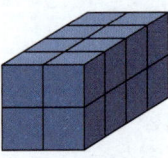

Volume = _____ cm³

Capacity = _____ ml

b)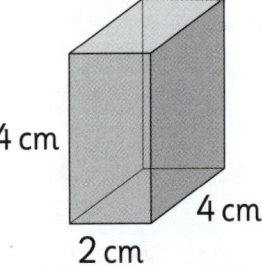

Volume = _____ cm³

Capacity = _____ ml

c)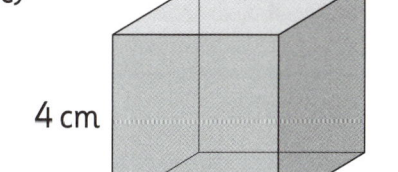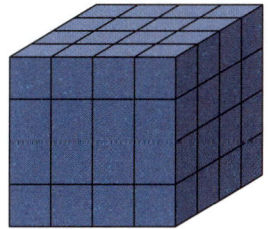

Volume = _____ cm³

Capacity = _____ ml

d)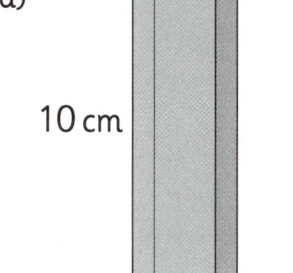

Volume = _____ cm³

Capacity = _____ ml

e)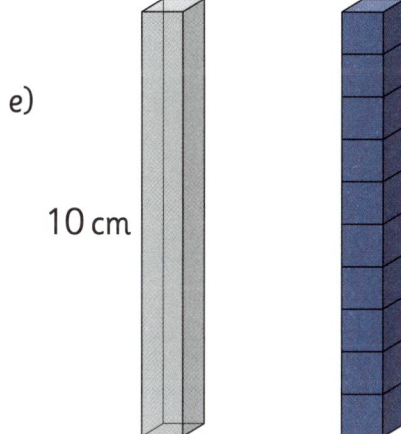

Volume = _____ cm³

Capacity = _____ ml

## ★ Challenge

Nuria builds a cube that is 10 cm by 10 cm by 10 cm.

I know that 10 × 10 × 10 is 1000. I know there are 100 cm in a m so there are 10 m³ in 1000 cm³. That means the volume of my cube is 10 m³.

Amman disagrees!

Is Nuria correct? Explain your reasoning.

## 9.5 Imperial measurement

**1** Convert these measurements of length. Fill in the spaces in the table.

| Metric | Imperial |
|---|---|
| 30 cm | 1 foot (12 inches) |
|  | 10 feet |
|  | 1 yard (3 feet) |
|  | 2 yards |
| 1·8 m | feet |

**2** Convert these measurements of mass. Fill in the spaces in the table.

| Metric | Imperial |
|---|---|
| 450 grams | 1 pound (16 ounces) |
|  | 0·5 pounds |
| 900 grams | ounces |
|  | 3 pounds |

**3** Convert these measurements of capacity. Fill in the spaces in the table.

| Metric | Imperial |
|---|---|
| **about** 500 ml | 1 pint (20 fluid ounces) |
| **about** | 10 fluid ounces |
|  | **about** 4 pints |
|  | **about** 8 pints (1 gallon) |
| 4000 ml |  |

4. Mrs Bing is 6 feet tall. Mrs Bong is 174 cm tall. Who is taller? How much taller? Show how you worked it out.

⭐ **Challenge**

Put these animals in weight order from heaviest to lightest. You can use a calculator!

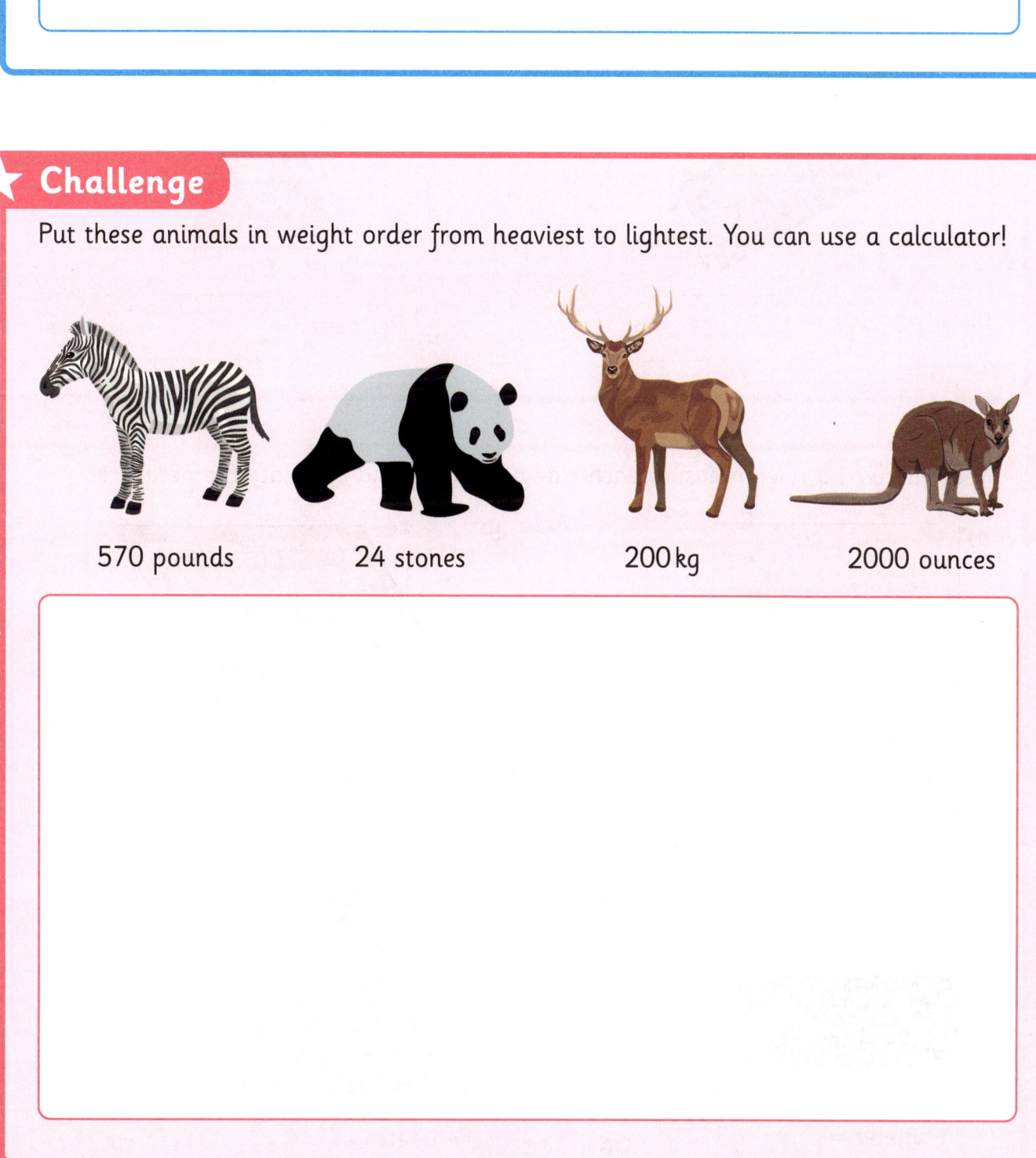

570 pounds     24 stones     200 kg     2000 ounces

# 9.6 Calculating perimeter

1) Calculate the perimeter of these shapes.

a)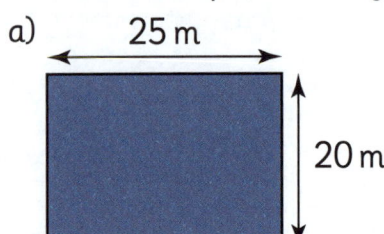

Perimeter = _____ m

b)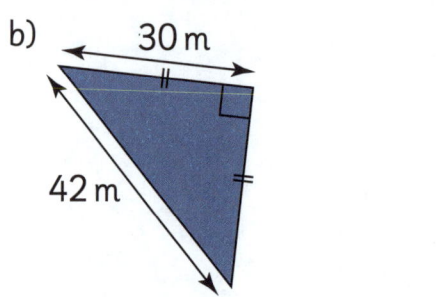

Perimeter = _____ m

c)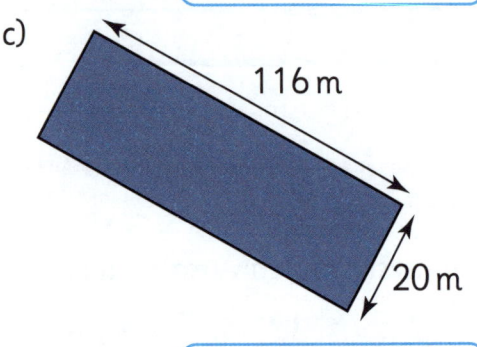

Perimeter = _____ m

d)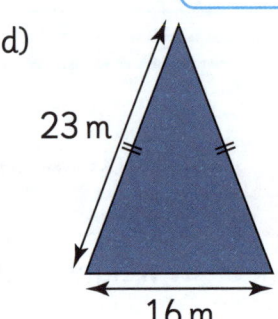

Perimeter = _____ m

2) You will need a ruler. Measure each side accurately and calculate the perimeter.

a)

Perimeter = _____ cm

b)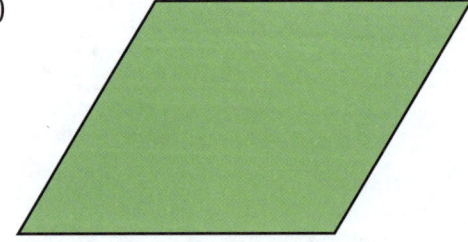

Perimeter = _____ cm

c)

Perimeter = _____ cm

d)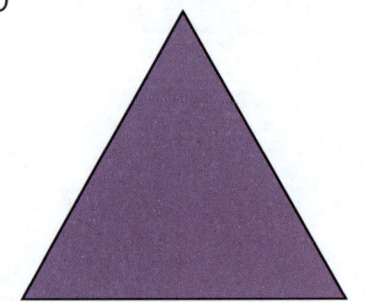

Perimeter = _____ cm

3) Estimate, then measure with a ruler and calculate the difference.

a)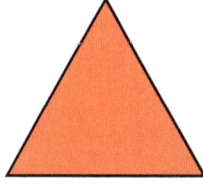

Estimate =

Actual =

Difference =

b)

Estimate =

Actual =

Difference =

c)

Estimate =

Actual =

Difference =

d)

Estimate =

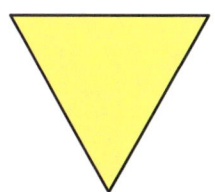

Actual =

Difference =

**Challenge**

Draw as many four-sided shapes as possible with a perimeter of 160 mm. Name each shape.

# 9.7 Calculating the area of regular shapes

1. Measure, then calculate the area of these rectangles.

   a)

   Area = ☐

   b)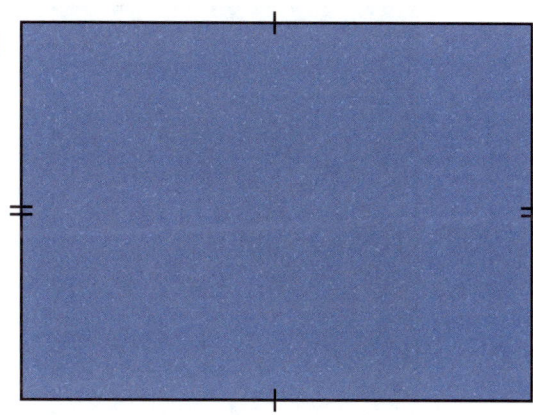

   Area = ☐

2. Draw triangles with areas of:
   a) 6 cm²
   b) 8 cm²
   c) 10 cm²

3) Draw in the lines to make each triangle into a rectangle. Calculate the area of the triangle.

a)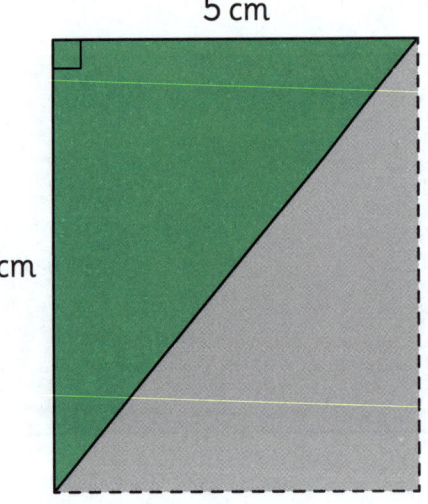

b)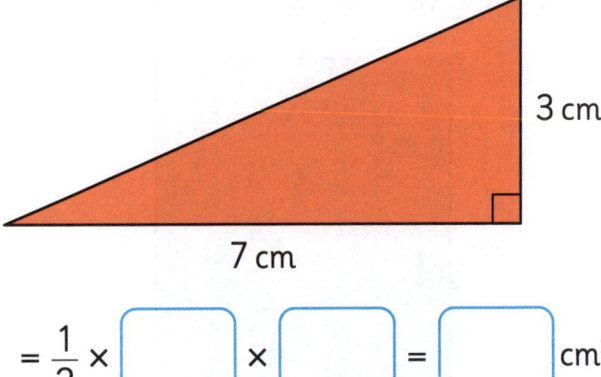

$= \dfrac{1}{2} \times \boxed{\phantom{0}} \times \boxed{\phantom{0}} = \boxed{\phantom{0}}$ cm²

Area $= \dfrac{1}{2} \times$ base $\times$ height

$= \dfrac{1}{2} \times \boxed{\phantom{0}} \times \boxed{\phantom{0}} = \boxed{\phantom{0}}$ cm²

c)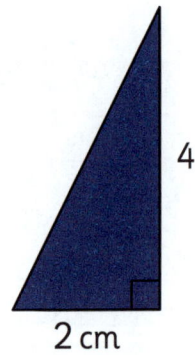

d)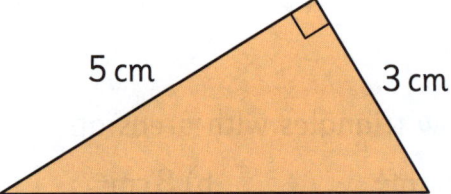

$= \dfrac{1}{2} \times \boxed{\phantom{0}} \times \boxed{\phantom{0}} = \boxed{\phantom{0}}$ cm²    $= \dfrac{1}{2} \times \boxed{\phantom{0}} \times \boxed{\phantom{0}} = \boxed{\phantom{0}}$ cm²

# Challenge

a) Draw a triangle that is **twice** the area of shape a.

b) Draw any shape that is **half** the area of shape b.

c) Draw a rectangle that is **half** the area and another rectangle that is a **quarter** the area of shape c.

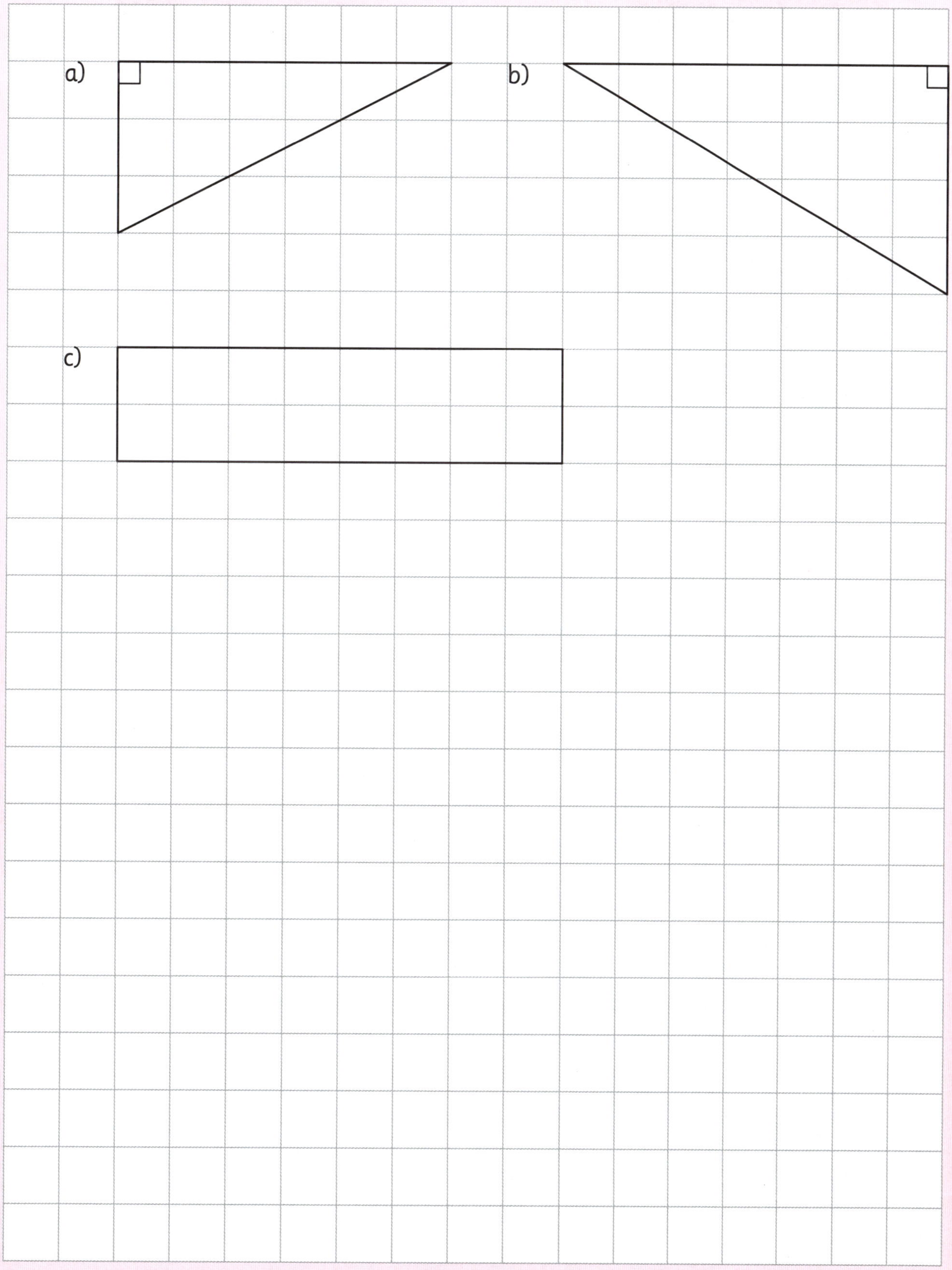

# 9.8 Calculating volume

**1)** Work out how many centimetre cubes make each of these cuboids.

a) ☐ cubic centimetres

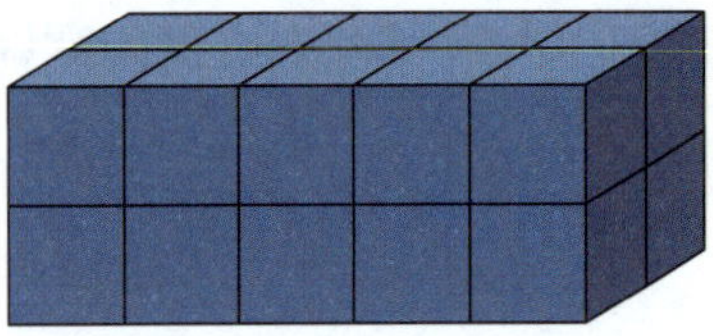

b) ☐ cubic centimetres

c) ☐ cubic centimetres

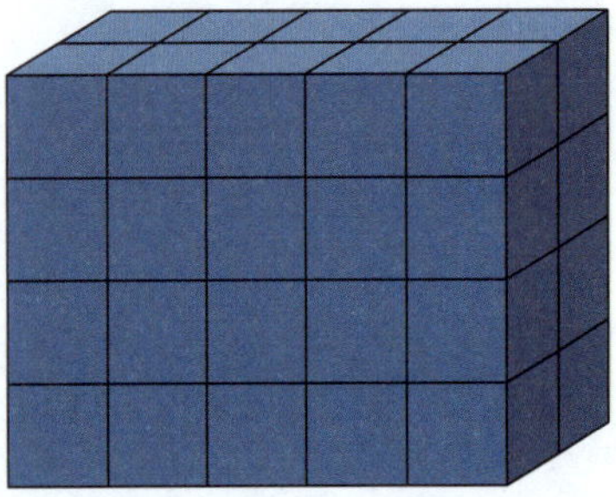

d) ☐ cubic centimetres

**2)** Amman builds cuboids with different volumes. Complete the table. The first one has been done for you.

| Volume of cuboid | Number of cubes on first layer | Number of layers |
|---|---|---|
| 18 cm³ | 9 | 2 |
| 20 cm³ |  | 5 |
| 25 cm³ |  | 1 |
| 28 cm³ | 7 |  |
| 56 cm³ |  |  |

3) We write cubic centimetres as cm³. Write down the volume of each of these cuboids. The diagrams are not to scale so calculate by counting the smaller cubes that make up the shapes.

a) 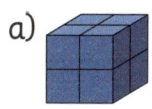   Volume = ☐ cm³

b)    Volume = ☐ cm³

c) 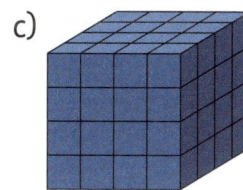   Volume = ☐ cm³

d)    Volume = ☐ cm³

## ★ Challenge

Nuria is building a model with 4 blocks. Her finished model has a volume of 170 cm³. What shape could block D be? Sketch your answer.

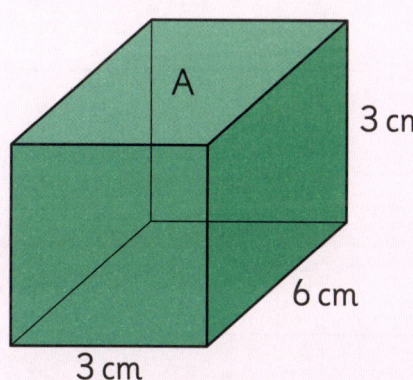

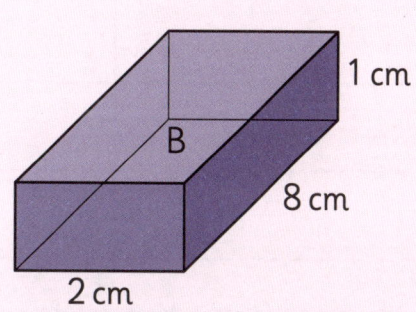

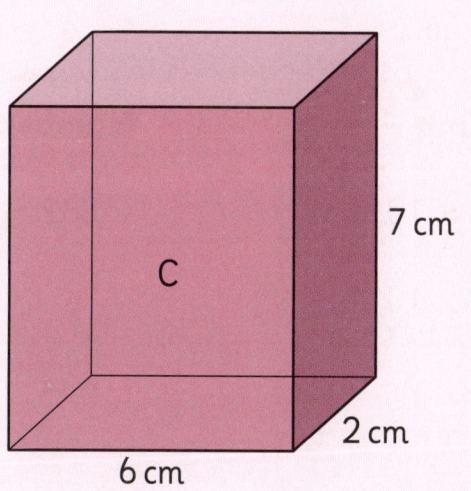

# 10.1 Mathematical inventions and different number systems

The Chinese number system uses symbols called **characters** to represent each number.

| 0 | zero | 零 |
|---|---|---|
| 1 | one | 一 |
| 2 | two | 二 |
| 3 | three | 三 |
| 4 | four | 四 |
| 5 | five | 五 |
| 6 | six | 六 |

| 7 | seven | 七 |
|---|---|---|
| 8 | eight | 八 |
| 9 | nine | 九 |
| 10 | ten | 十 |
| 100 | one hundred | 百 |
| 1000 | one thousand | 千 |
| 10 000 | ten thousand | 万 |

**1** The Chinese number system shows how many tens there are first. Complete the table. The first one is done for you.

| Chinese Characters | Meaning | Number |
|---|---|---|
| 八十五 | 8 × 10, 5 | 85 |
|  | 3 × 10, 1 |  |
|  |  | 76 |
| 四十九 |  |  |

**2** The hundreds numbers are written by putting the number of hundreds first. Complete the table. The first one is done for you.

| Chinese Characters | Meaning | Number |
|---|---|---|
| 八百三十二 | 8 × 100, 3 × 10, 2 | 832 |
|  | 9 × 100, 2 × 10, 1 |  |
|  |  | 634 |
| 二百九十五 |  |  |

**3** The thousands numbers are written by putting the number of thousands first. Complete the table. The first one is done for you.

| Chinese Characters | Meaning | Number |
|---|---|---|
| 四千三百五十六 | 4 × 1000, 3 × 100, 5 × 10, 6 | 4356 |
| 七千八百五十九 | | |
| | | 2163 |
| | 3 × 1000, 2 × 100, 6 × 10, 8 | |

**4** Use the Chinese characters 一, 二, 三, 十, 百.

Use each character once to make 5-digit numbers. How many different 5-digit numbers can you make?

## ★ Challenge

Complete these calculations and give your answers in Chinese characters.

a) 三百四十四 + 二十二 = 

b) 六百七十八 + 四 = 

c) 六千三百五十一 + ⬚ = 六千四百五十一

# 11.1 Exploring and extending number sequences

**1** a) In the bakery, each cake has 6 chocolate buttons on top.
Complete the table to show the pattern.

| No. of cakes (c)   | 1 | 2 | 3 | 4 | 5 |
|--------------------|---|---|---|---|---|
| No. of buttons (b) | 6 |   |   |   |   |

b) Write the pattern you notice in words.

c) The number of buttons is ☐ × the number of cakes.

d) Complete the formula b = ☐ × ☐

**2** a) In the garden centre each tub has 8 flowers in it.
Complete the table to show the pattern.

| No. of tubs (t)    | 1 | 2 | 3 | 4 | 5 |
|--------------------|---|---|---|---|---|
| No. of flowers (f) | 8 |   |   |   |   |

b) The number of flowers is ☐ × ☐

c) Write the formula in symbols ☐

d) Use the formula to work out how many flowers there would be if there were 12 tubs.

3. a) Each heptagon is made of 7 matchsticks. Complete the table to show the pattern.

| No. of heptagons (h) | 1 | 2 | 3 | 4 | 5 |
|---|---|---|---|---|---|
| No. of matchsticks (m) | 7 | | | | |

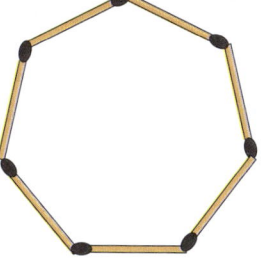

b) Write the formula.

c) Use the formula to work out how many matchsticks there would be if there were 20 heptagons.

## ★ Challenge

Nuria's dog ate part of her homework. Complete the table.

| Cards (C) | | | | | | | | | 9 | 10 |
|---|---|---|---|---|---|---|---|---|---|---|
| Stamps (S) | | | | | | | | | 36 | 40 |

b) Write the formula here:

# 12.1 Solving equations using mathematical rules

**1** Use one of these symbols < > = ≠ to make each of these statements true. Each symbol must be used once only.

a) 156 + 4  ☐  160 ÷ 4

b) 156 + 40  ☐  200 − 4

c) 686 − 120  ☐  526 + 50

d) 567 + 120  ☐  526 − 50

**2** Choose one of these calculations to balance each equation. Each calculation must be used at least once.

24 × 1    12 × 1    6 × 2    6 × 4

a) 4 × 6 = ☐

b) 3 × 8 = ☐

c) 48 ÷ 2 = ☐

d) 4 × 3 = ☐

e) 36 ÷ 3 = ☐

f) $\frac{1}{2}$ of 48 = ☐

**3** Find the missing number in each equation.

a) ☐ − 4 = 3 × 5

b) 15 + ☐ = 25 − 6

c) 25 × 2 = ☐ × 10

d) 50 ÷ 10 = 60 − ☐

e) 55 ÷ 11 = ☐ ÷ 5

f) ☐ + 50 = $\frac{3}{4}$ of 100

★ **Challenge**

Each shape represents a number. Work out what each of these shapes represents.

 = 10

 = 13

□ ● ● ● = 9

□ ● ▲ ▲ = 15

 = 14

Jottings

# 13.1 Naming and sorting shapes

**1** A regular polygon has congruent sides and angles. What does this mean?

**2** Are these shapes **regular** or **irregular**? Write each letter in the correct box.

| regular polygon | irregular polygon |
|---|---|

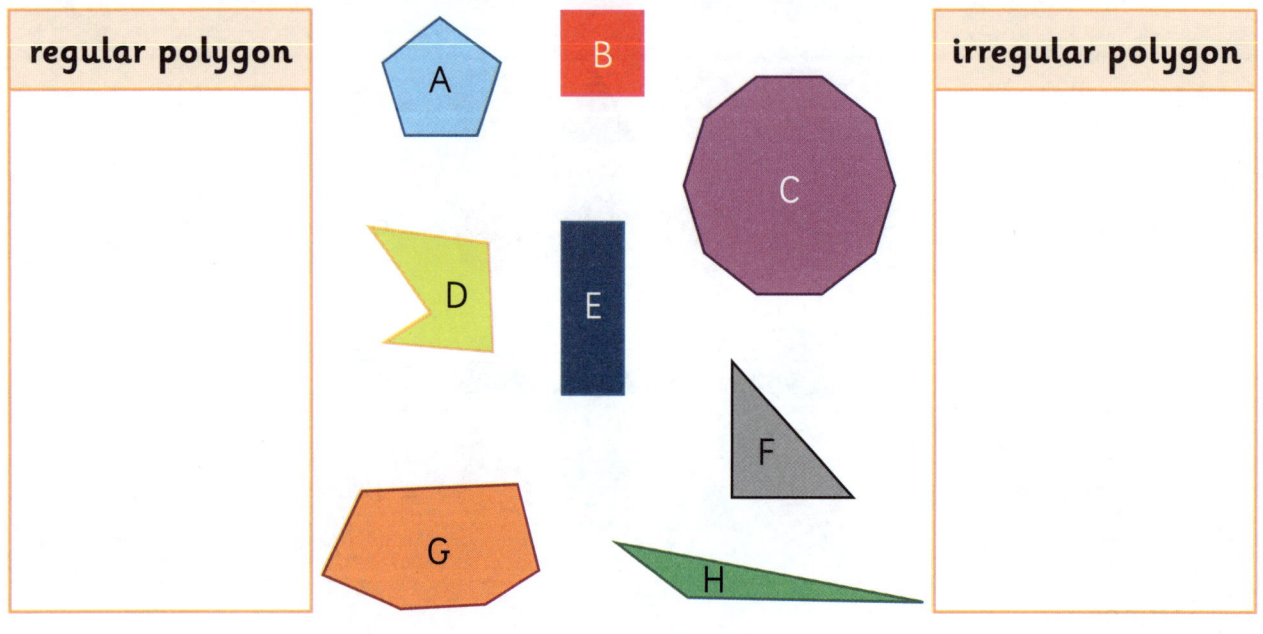

**3** Draw and then name these shapes. Make sure to say if the shapes are **regular** or **irregular**.

a) I have three straight sides.

My sides are different lengths.

I have three vertices.

b) I have four straight sides.

Two of my sides are different lengths.

I have four vertices.

c) I have six straight sides.

My sides are the same length.

I have six vertices.

d) I have five straight sides.

My sides are different lengths.

I have five vertices.

## ⭐ Challenge

a) Look at these shapes. Decide how to sort them and put them into two groups. Label your groups to show your criteria.

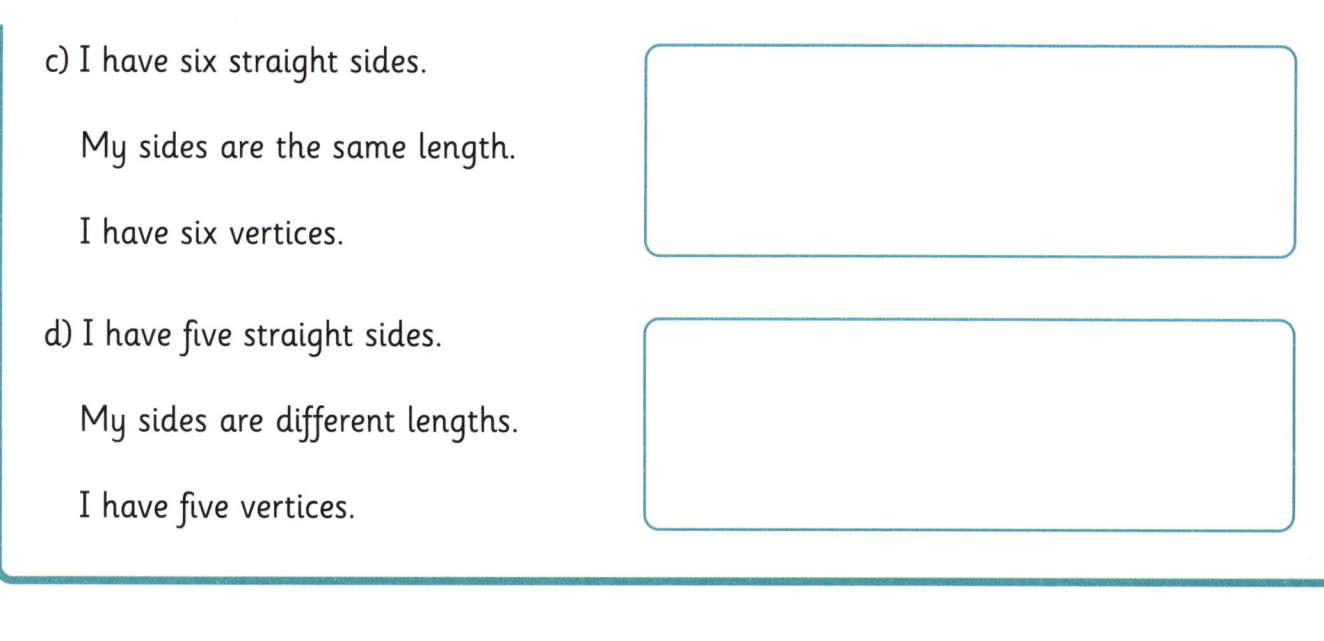

**Group 1**

Label:

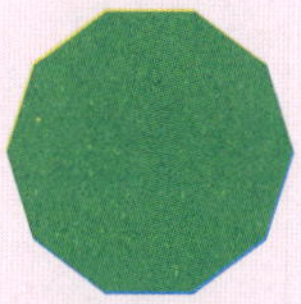

**Group 2**

Label:

## 13.2 Describing and drawing circles

**1** Label the diameter, radius and circumference of this circle.

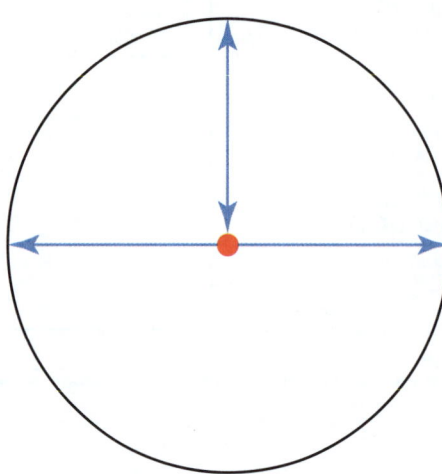

**2** a) Use a pair of compasses to draw a circle with a radius of 4 cm and a circle with a diameter of 6 cm. Your circles can overlap.

b) Measure the diameter and radius of both of your circles.

Circle 1 diameter = 

Circle 1 radius = 

Circle 2 diameter = 

Circle 2 radius =

**3** Complete the table.

| Shape | Radius | Diameter | Approximate circumference |
|---|---|---|---|
| A | 11 cm | | |
| B | | 44 cm | |
| C | | | 120 mm |
| D | | 38 cm | |
| E | 18 m | | |

## ★ Challenge

Create a design using four circles. Use a pair of compasses. First, draw a circle that has a radius of 2 cm. Now add a circle with a diameter of 8 cm. Then add a circle with an approximate circumference of 30 cm. Finally, add a circle of your choosing.

# 13.3 Constructing 3D objects

1. Match each skeleton to the correct name.

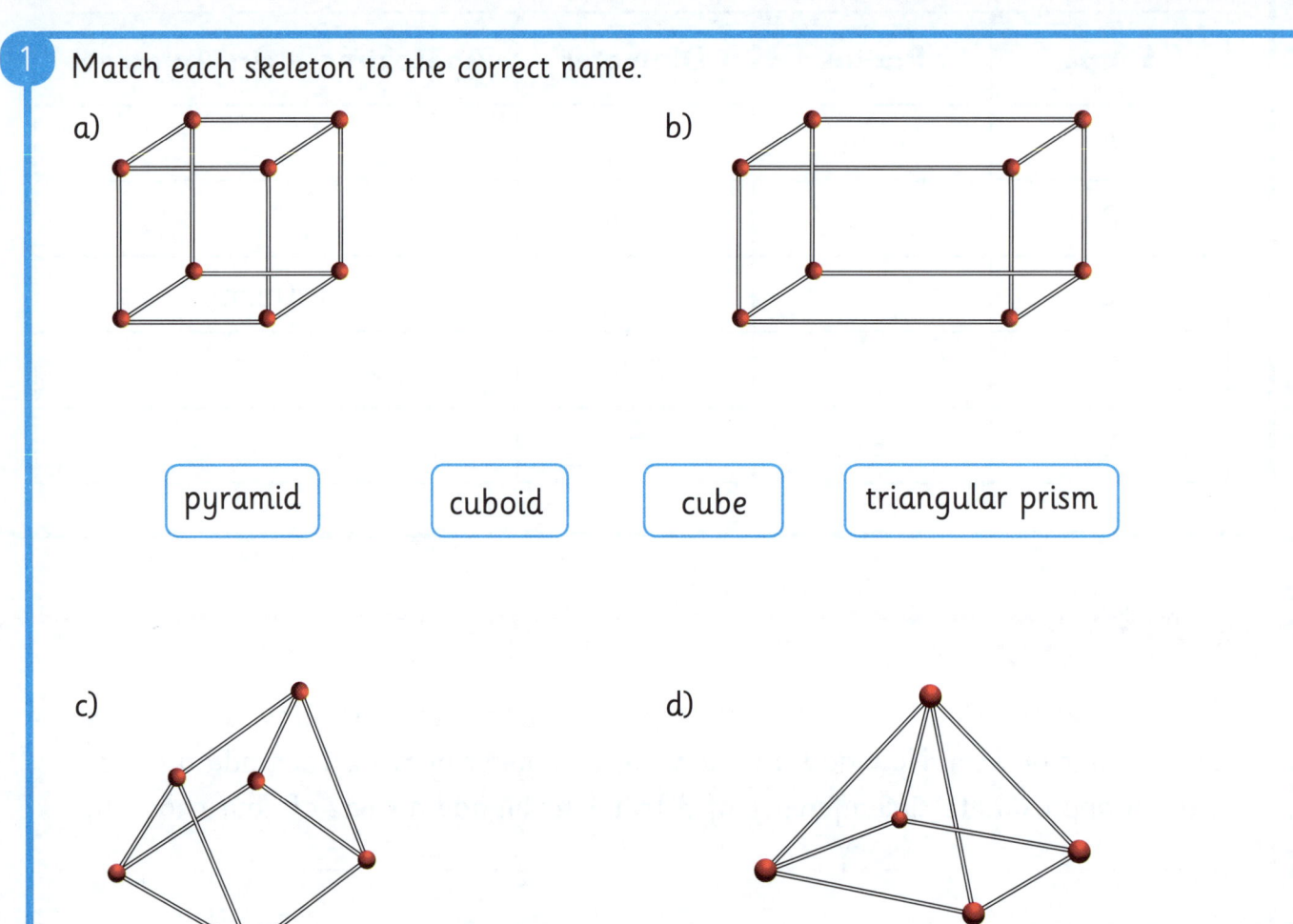

pyramid    cuboid    cube    triangular prism

2. Find examples of 3D objects to help you complete the table. Answer yes or no. The first one is done for you.

| Object | More than two edges meeting at a vertex | Can have a square face |
|---|---|---|
| cuboid | Yes | Yes |
| pyramid | | |
| cylinder | | |

78

3) Draw in all the missing edges in each of these and write the name of the 3D object underneath.

a)

b)

c)

d)

## ★ Challenge

You will need scissors, straws and sticky tape or modelling clay.

a) Use four long straws and eight short straws to build a cuboid. Sketch it here:

How many vertices does it have? ☐

b) Remove two short straws and one long straw from your cuboid and create a triangular prism from the remaining skeleton. Sketch it here:

How many vertices does it have? ☐

c) Remove three short straws from your triangular prism and create a triangular based pyramid from the remaining skeleton. Sketch it here:

How many vertices does it have? ☐

# 13.4 Constructing nets

**1**

**You will need centimetre squared paper.**

a) Copy this net onto the centimetre squared paper.

I predict this net will fold into a 3D object called a ☐

b) Cut out your net, fold and create the 3D object.

My object is a ☐

**2**

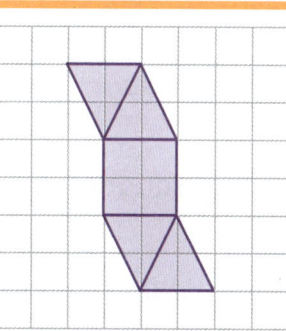

a) Copy this net onto the centimetre squared paper.

I predict this net will fold into a 3D object called a ☐

b) Cut out your net, fold and create the 3D object.

My object is a ☐

**3**

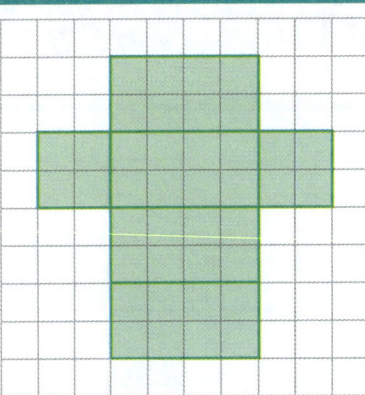

a) Copy this net onto the centimetre squared paper.

I predict this net will fold into a 3D object called a ☐

b) Cut out your net, fold and create the 3D object.

My object is a ☐

**4**

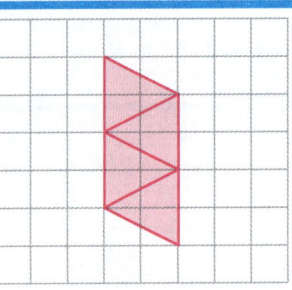

a) Copy this net onto the centimetre squared paper.

I predict this net will fold into a 3D object called a ☐

b) Cut out your net, fold and create the 3D object.

My object is a ☐

**Challenge**

You will need:
- Squared paper if you run out of space here!
- A ruler

Make as many different nets of a triangular prism as you can. Draw them here:

# 14.1 Identifying and sorting angles

1. Match these angles to the correct name and description.

| | | |
|---|---|---|
| exactly 90° | | acute |
| less than 90° | | reflex |
| exactly 180° | | right |
| more than 180° | | straight |
| more than 90°, less than 180° | | obtuse |

2. Sort these angles and complete the table. One has been done for you.

| Acute | Obtuse | Reflex |
|---|---|---|
| a) | | |
| | | |

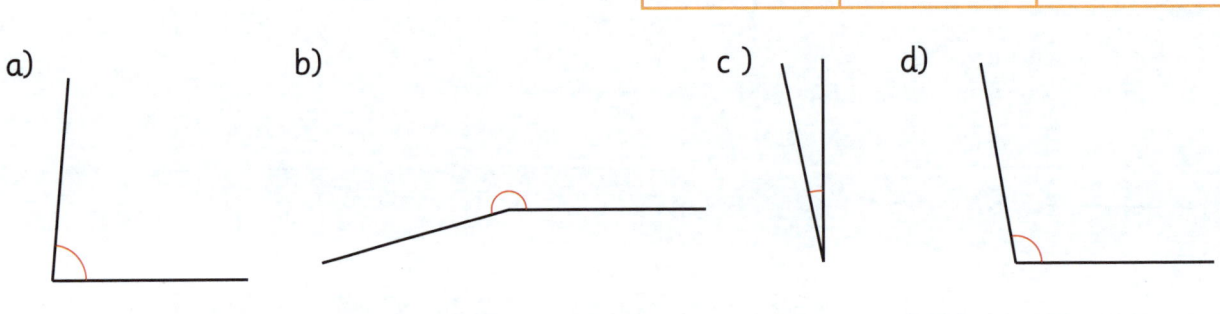

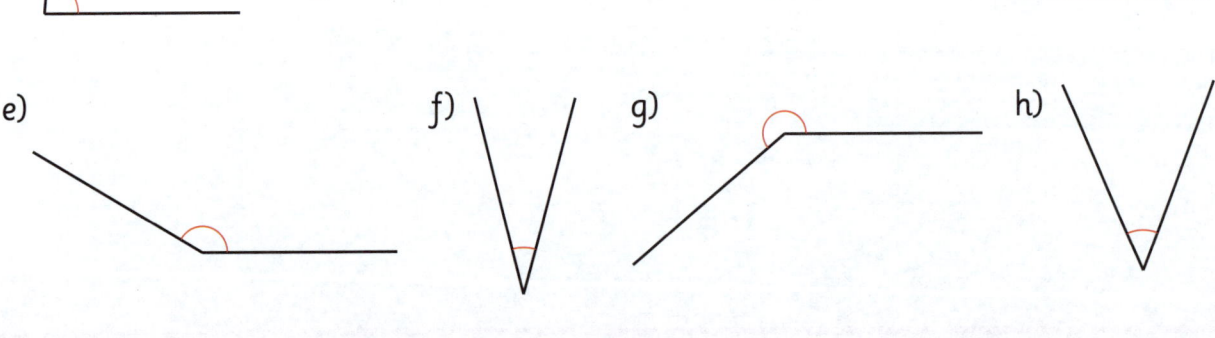

3) Correct the children's work. Tick the correctly identified angles and put a cross at the incorrect ones.

Amman (reflex angles):

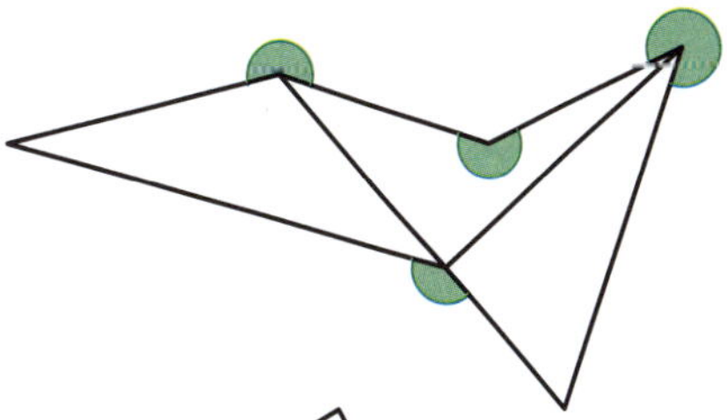

Nuria (obtuse angles):

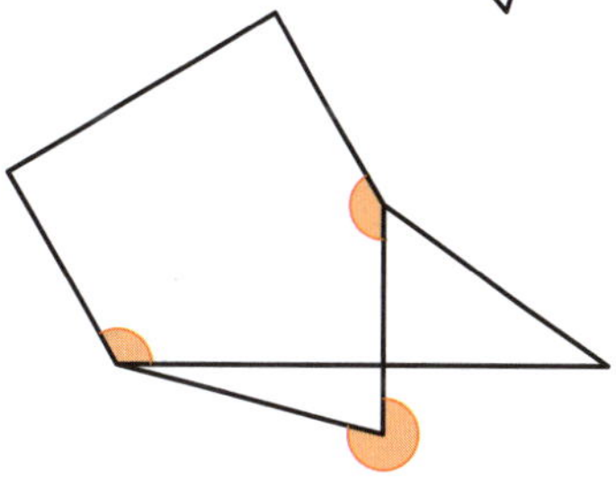

Isla (acute angles):

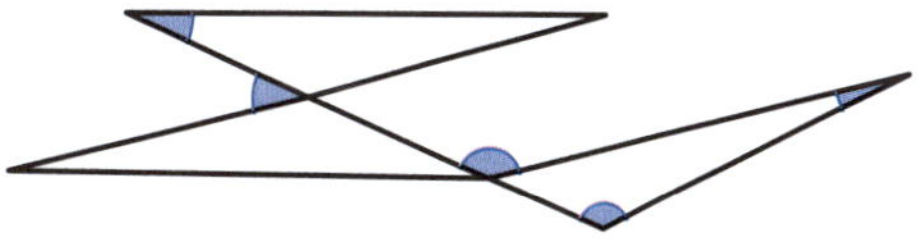

## ★ Challenge

Draw a 2D shape that matches these instructions.

1. Has three right angles and two obtuse angles.

2. Has two obtuse angles and two acute angles.

3. Has one right angle, one acute angle and two obtuse angles.

# 14.2 Measuring and drawing angles

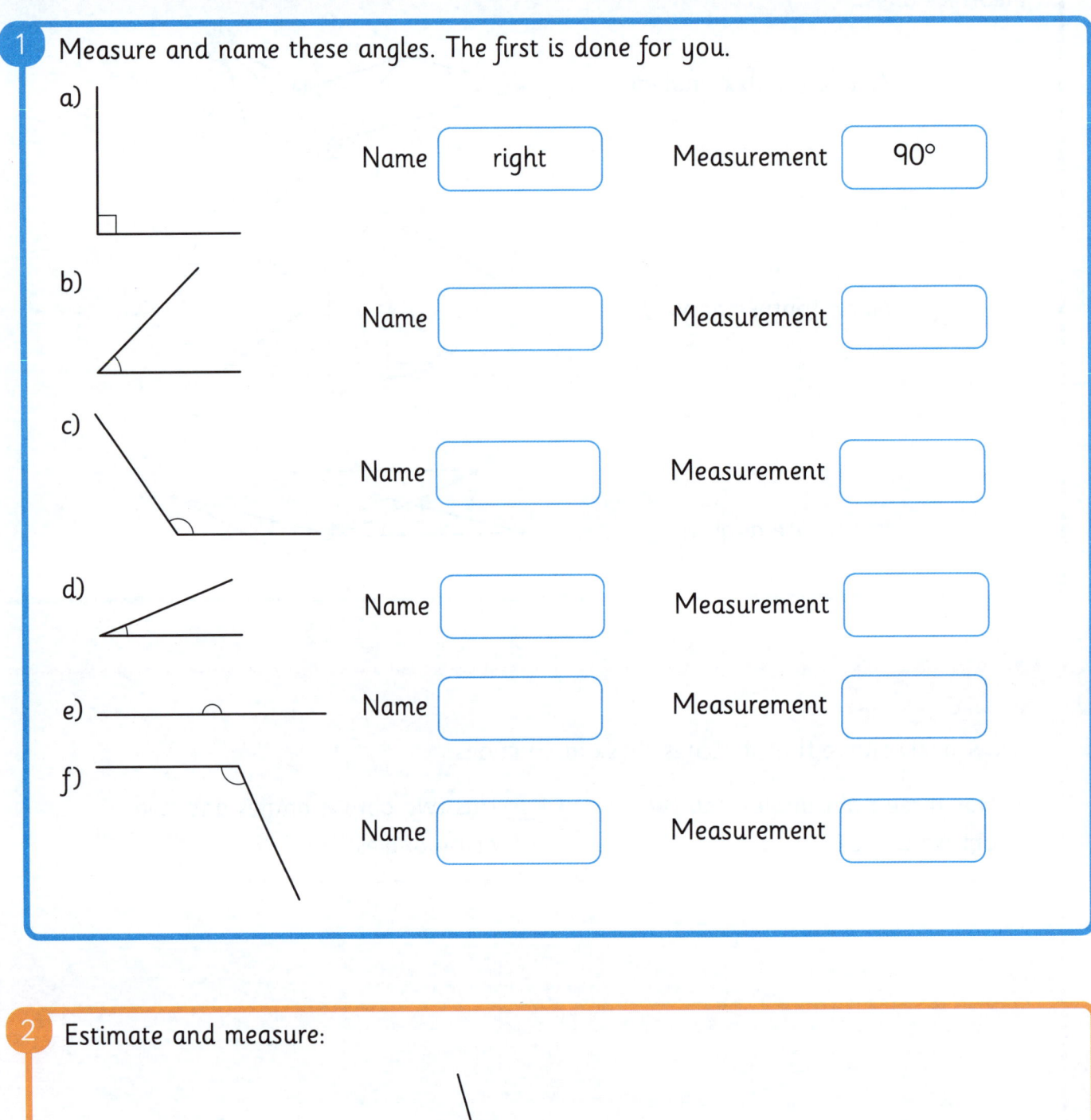

1. Measure and name these angles. The first is done for you.

a) Name: right   Measurement: 90°

b) Name: ___   Measurement: ___

c) Name: ___   Measurement: ___

d) Name: ___   Measurement: ___

e) Name: ___   Measurement: ___

f) Name: ___   Measurement: ___

2. Estimate and measure:

Estimate: ___   Measurement: ___

**3** Draw and label these angles using a protractor on the line below.

a) 56°  b) 156°  c) 256°

---

★ **Challenge**

Find and write the names of 5 different four-sided shapes with inside angles that total 360°.

Now draw them accurately below.

# 14.3 Finding missing angles

1) Match the definition to the name.

Two angles that add up to 90°

complementary          supplementary

Two angles that add up to 180°

2) Calculate the missing complementary angles.

a) 15°, A  ☐

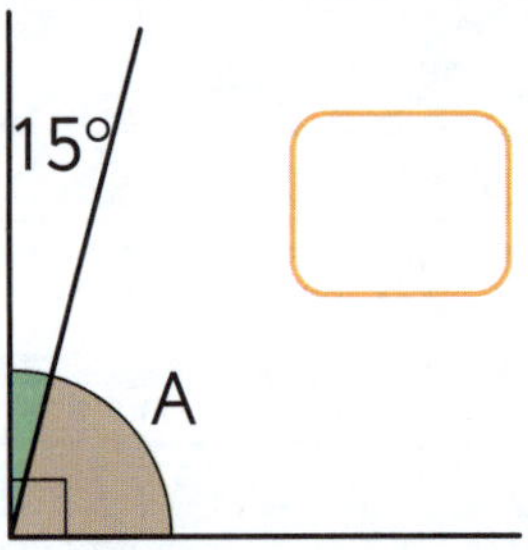

b) 54°, B  ☐

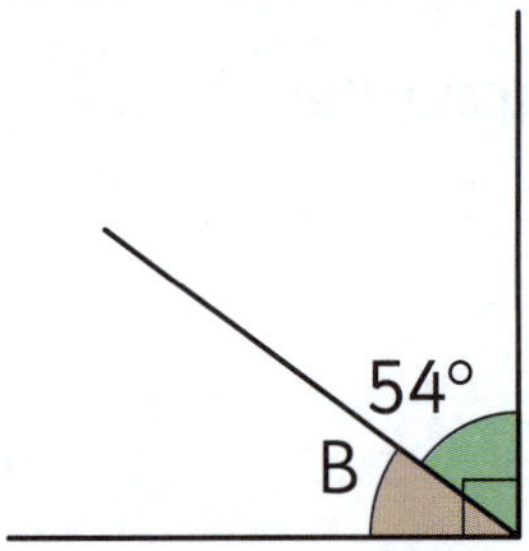

c) 74°, C  ☐

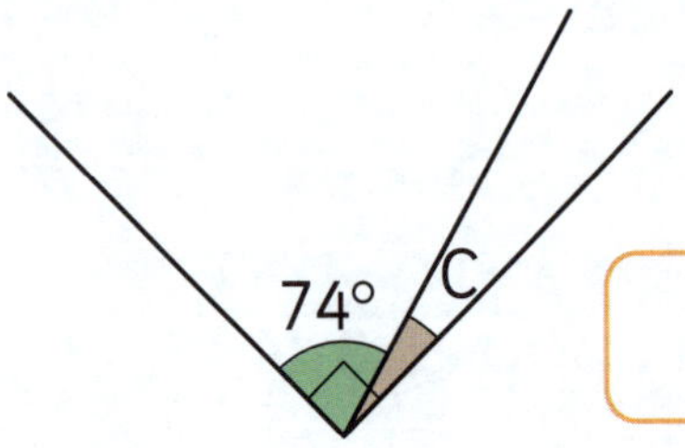

d) D, 19°  ☐

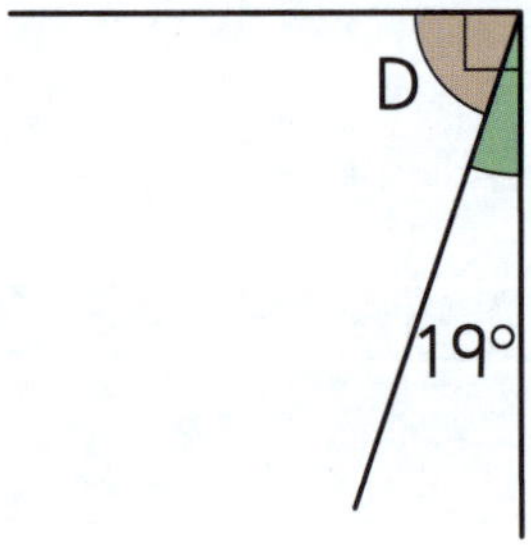

e) E, 62°  ☐

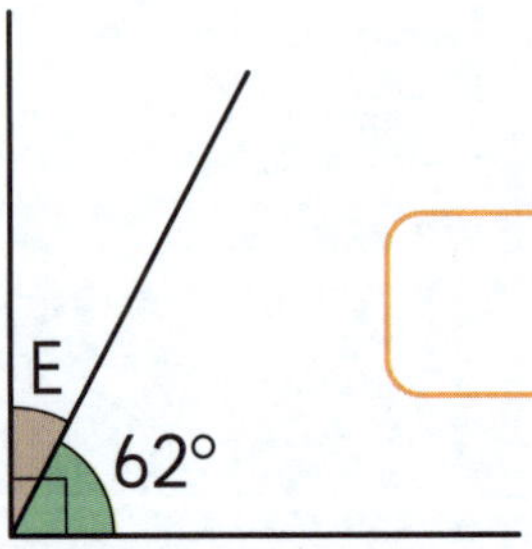

f) F, 23°  ☐

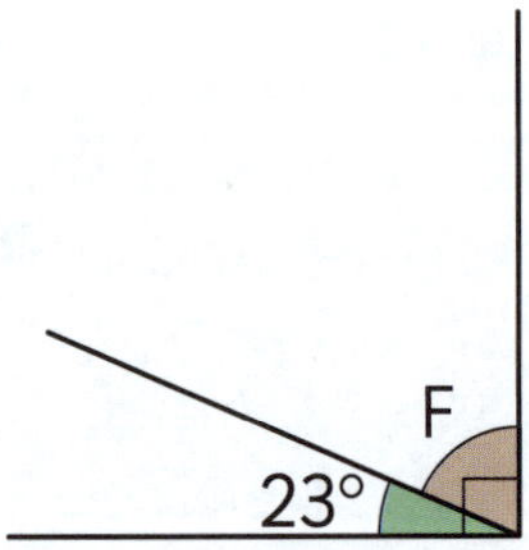

**3** Calculate the missing complementary angles.

a)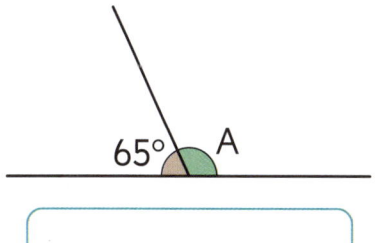

b)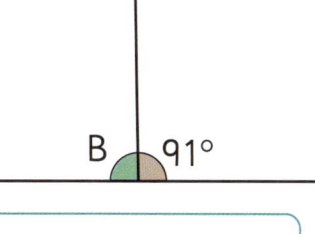

c)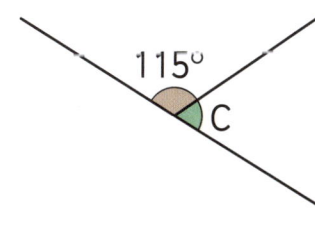

d)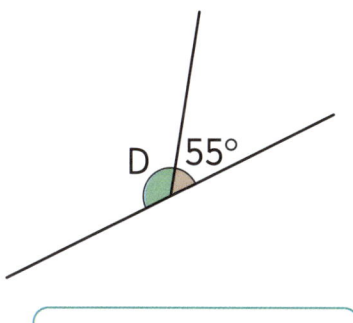

e)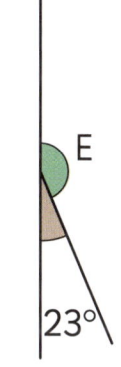

f)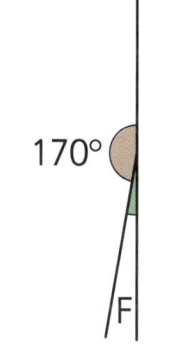

**4** Measure and find the missing angles.

a)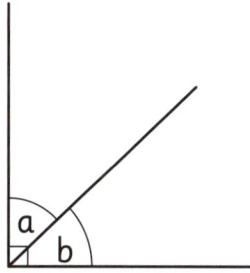

b)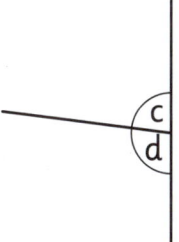

c)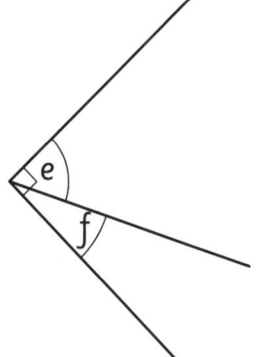

Measure angle a = ☐    Measure angle c = ☐    Measure angle e = ☐

Calculate angle b = ☐    Calculate angle d = ☐    Calculate angle f = ☐

## Challenge

This is a Frayer model for right angles:

| Definition | Characteristics |
|---|---|
| An angle that measures 90° | The angle created when two straight lines are perpendicular to each other. |
| Example | Non example |

Create a Frayer model for complementary angles.

| Definition | Characteristics |
|---|---|
| | |
| Example | Non example |

Create a Frayer model for supplementary angles.

| Definition | Characteristics |
|---|---|
| | |
| Example | Non example |

# 14.4 Locating objects using bearings

**1** Complete the compass rose with 3-figure bearings.

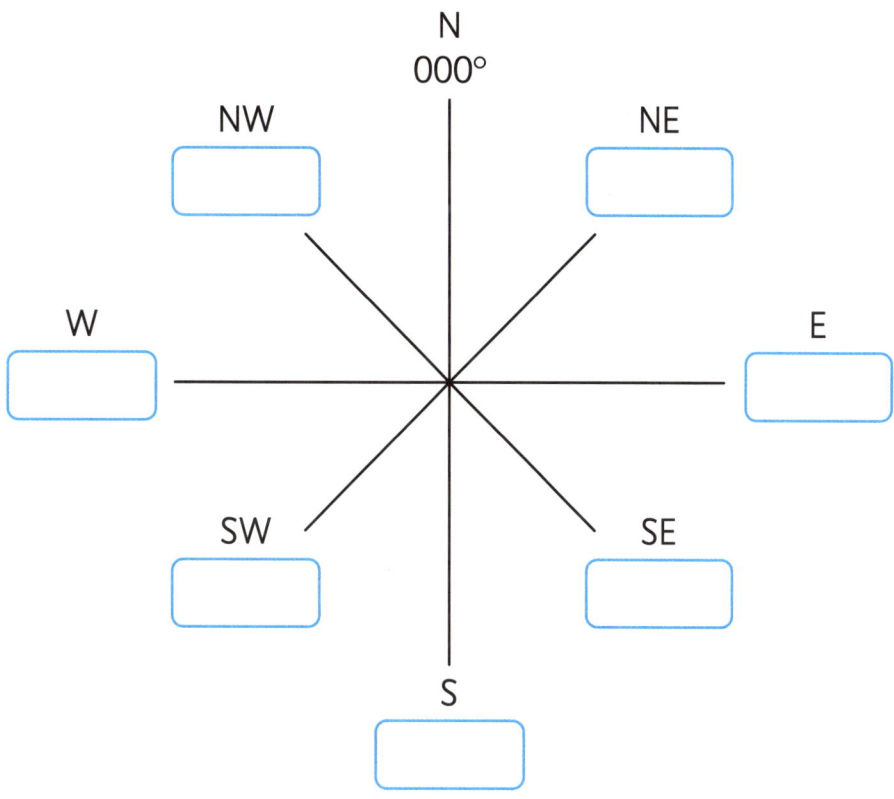

**2** Complete the table by ticking the correct answer.

|  | True | False | Do not know |
|---|---|---|---|
| Bearings must always have 3 digits |  |  |  |
| It is possible to have bearings over 360° |  |  |  |
| Bearings are used in map reading |  |  |  |
| Bearings start at either North, South, East or West |  |  |  |

Write your own fact about bearings here. Ask a partner to answer true / false / do not know. Are they correct?

3

Major cities within the British Isles

You will need a protractor or angle measure. Ms Keith is a pilot. She needs to use bearings to know which direction to fly in. Complete the table to show bearings from these airports.

| From | To | Bearing |
| --- | --- | --- |
| Glasgow | Aberdeen | |
| Aberdeen | Newcastle upon Tyne | |
| Edinburgh | Belfast | |
| London | Cardiff | |
| Bristol | Glasgow | |

**Challenge**

Create an imaginary map below. It can be anywhere in the world! Put six landmarks on your map and mark them A, B, C, D, E and F. Create a tour for a visitor to your area. Give them instructions below your map.

| From | To | Bearing |
|---|---|---|
| A | B | |
| B | C | |
| C | D | |
| D | E | |
| E | F | |

# 14.5 Reading coordinates

**1** Write down the coordinates of the vertices of each shape.

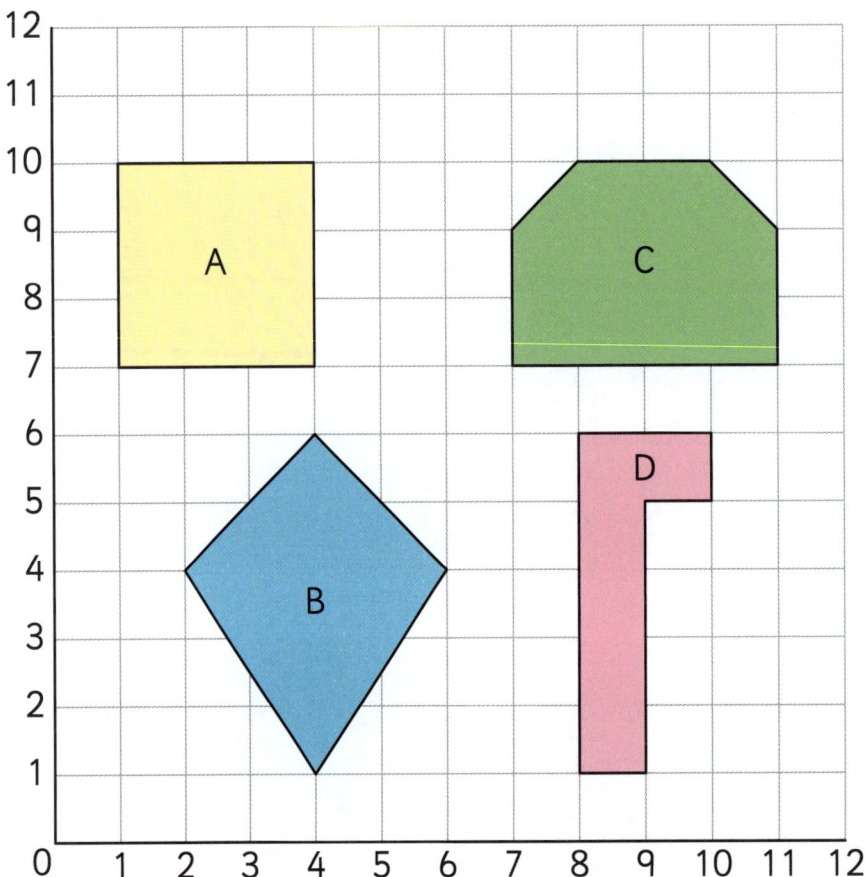

a)

b)

c)

d)

2. a) Plot the following coordinates. Join the dots to reveal the image.

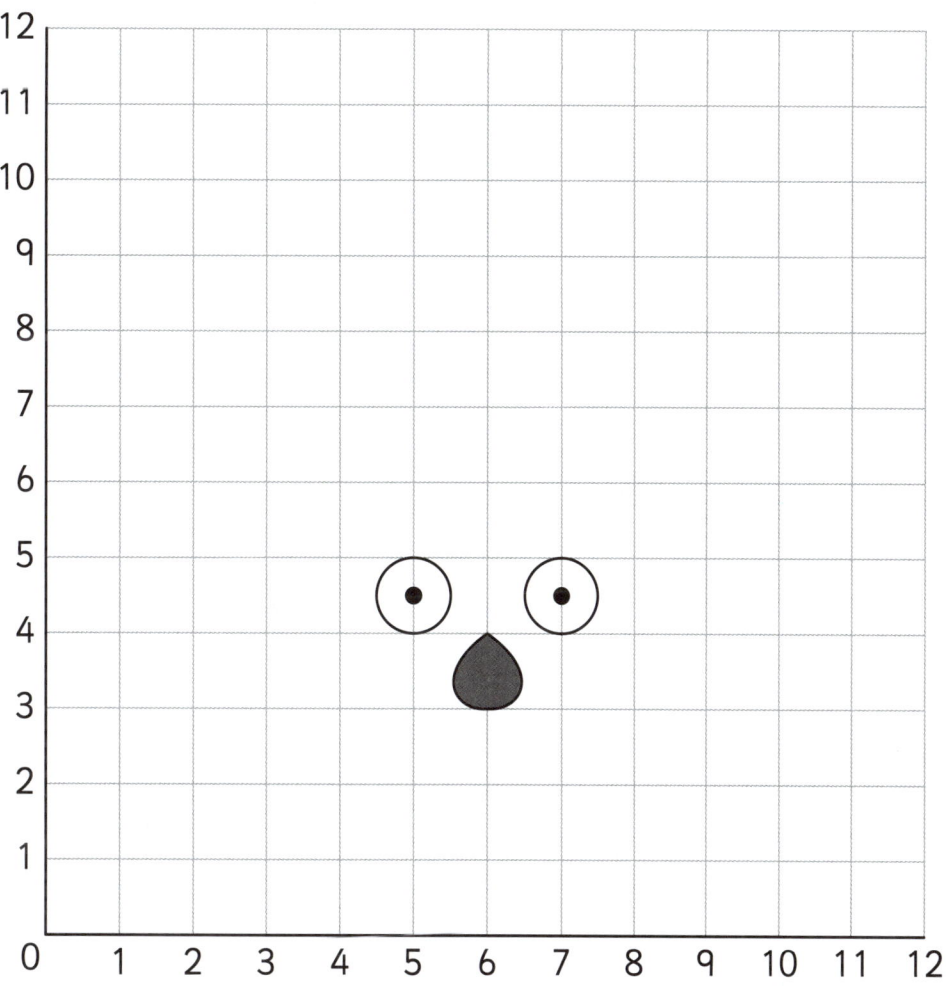

(4,11), (3,9), (3,7), (2,6), (2,2), (5,1), (7,1), (10,2), (10,6), (9,7), (9,9), (8,11), (7,9), (7,7), (5,7), (5,9)

b) Add in six whiskers and write the coordinates here:

**3** Identify the missing coordinates in these shapes. Draw them on the grid.

a) Square (1,6), (1,10) (5, 10)

b) Rectangle (12,5), (12,7) (6,5)

c) Square (2,1), (10,1) (10,9)

d) Rectangle (2,2), (2,4) (8,4)

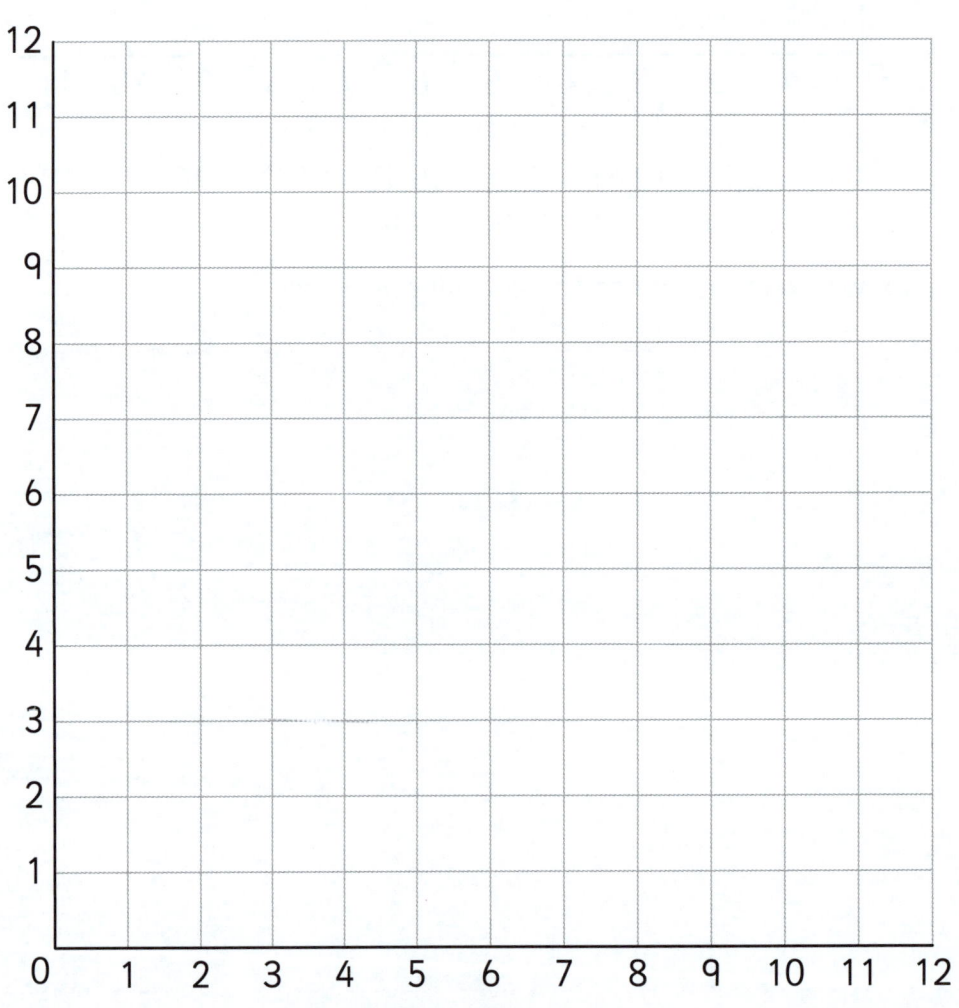

## ★ Challenge

You are going to create an image using the first letter of your first name and the first letter of your surname. You must try to fill the space so your letters will overlap. An example is shown here using K and H:

(1,0), (2,0), (6,0), (7,0), (7,11), (6,11), (6,6), (6,5), (2,11), (1,11) (2,6), (2,5)

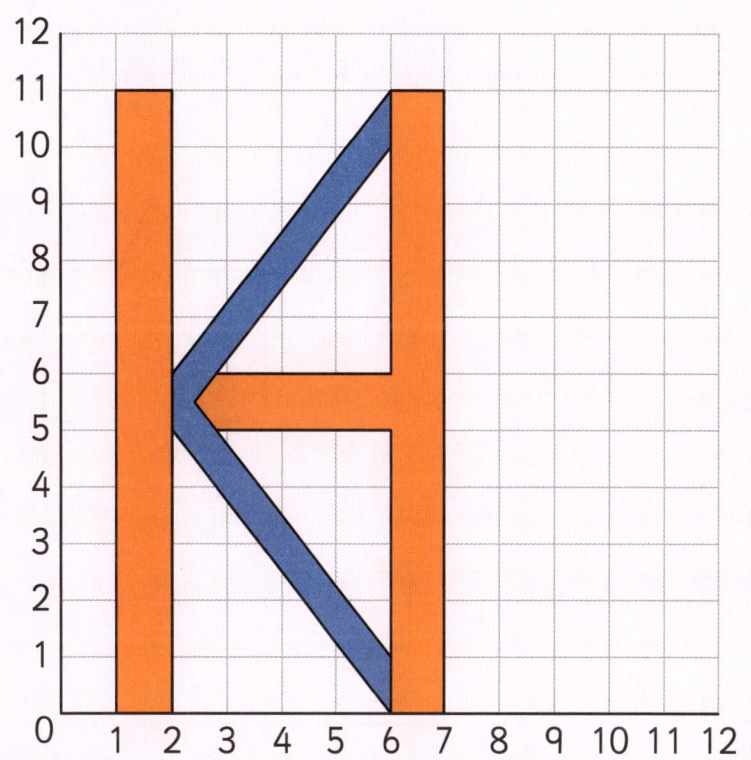

Colour your design and write the coordinates in the box:

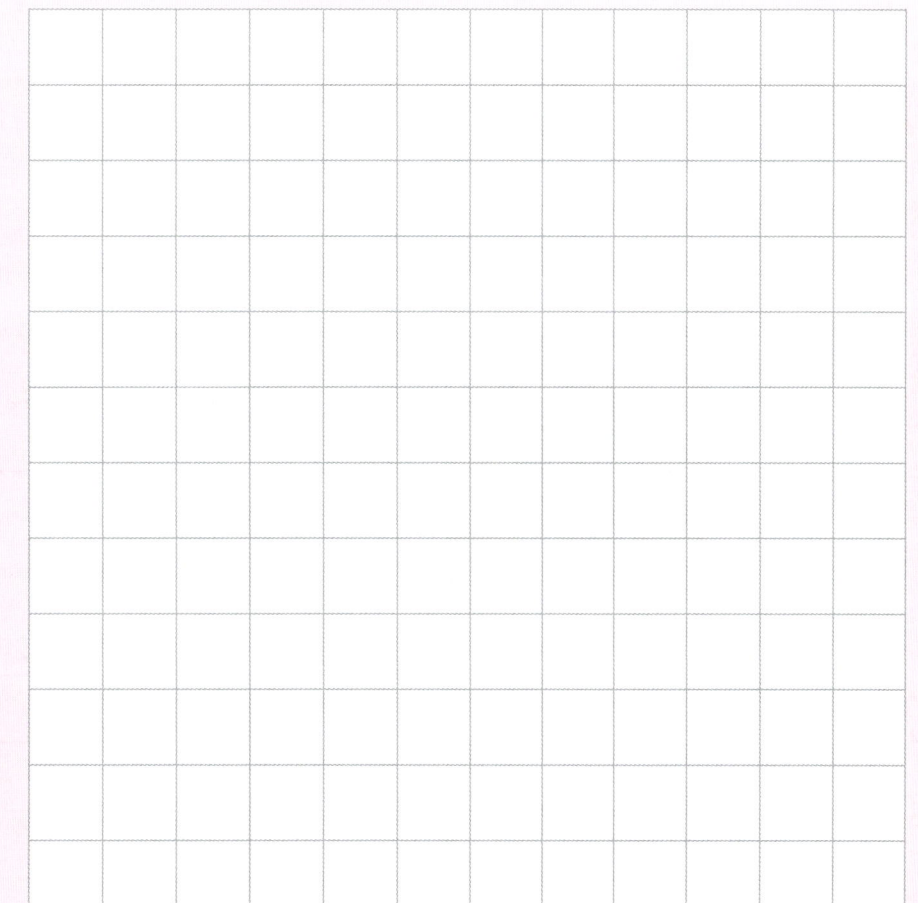

# 14.6 Line symmetry

1. Draw two lines of symmetry on each shape.

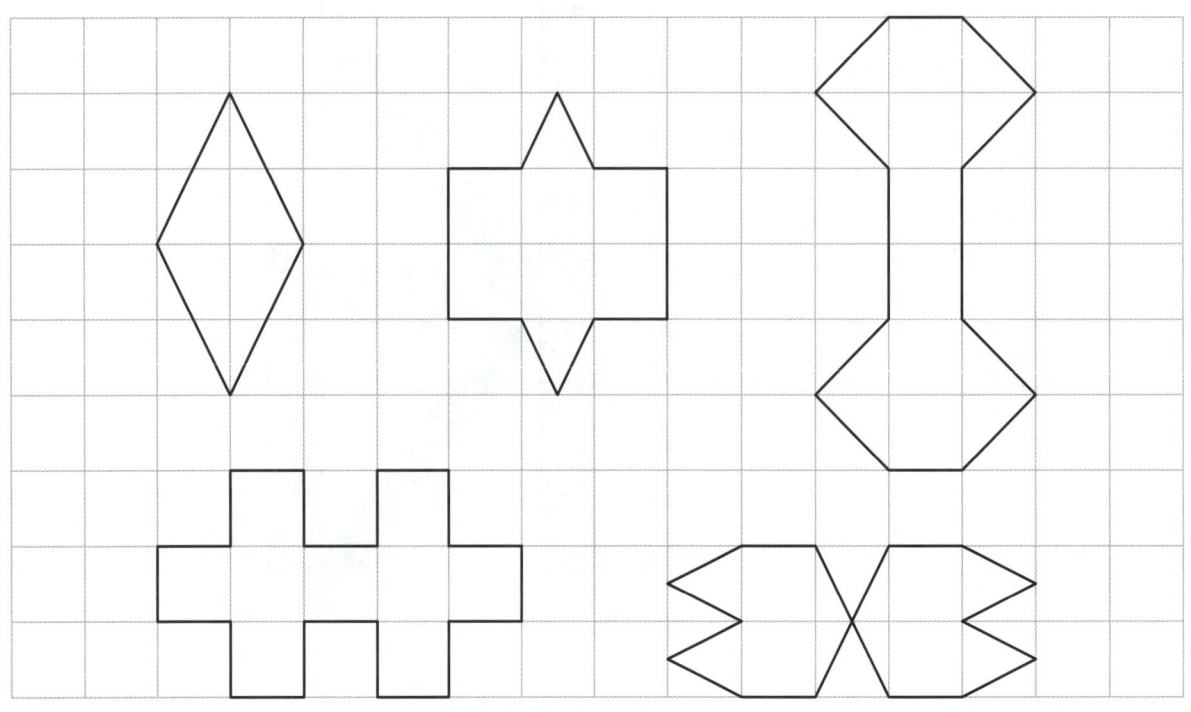

2. You must use three different colours. Colour the squares so that each one has two lines of symmetry. An example is shown below. You could use a mirror to check your designs.

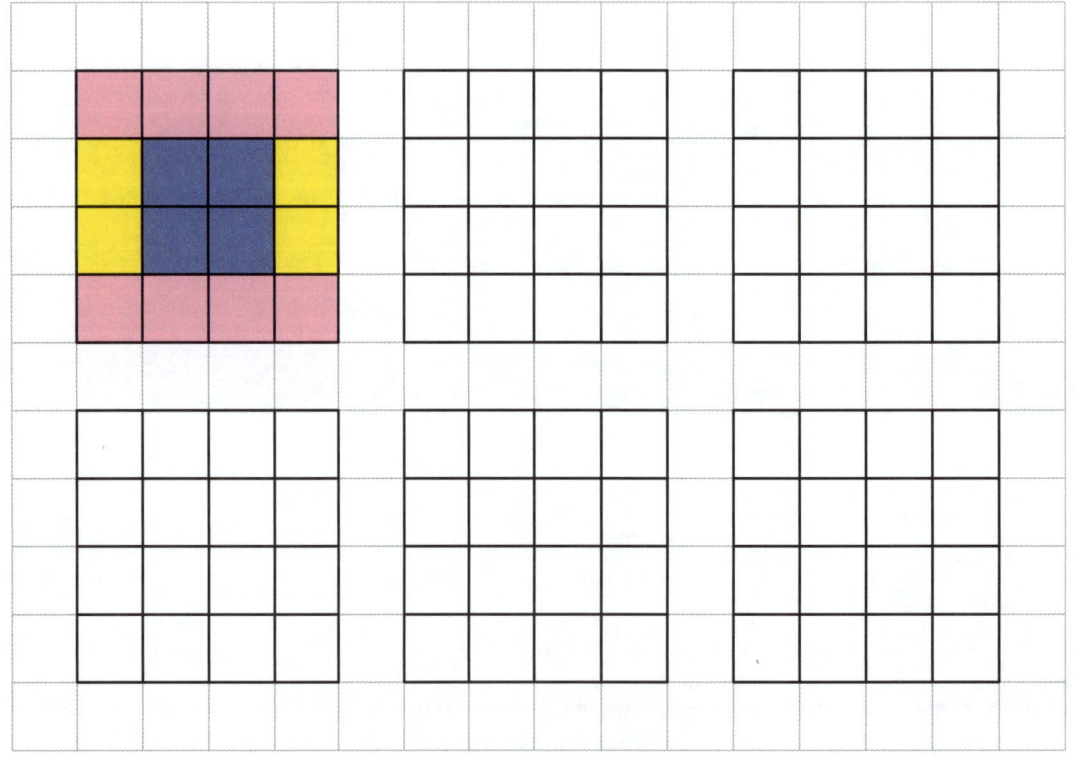

3) Look at these designs. Complete the table.

a) b) c) d)

e) f) g) h)

| No lines of symmetry | One line of symmetry | Two or more lines of symmetry |
|---|---|---|
|  |  |  |
|  |  |  |
|  |  |  |

### ★ Challenge

**You will need a piece of card measuring 3 cm by 3 cm and a sheet of paper.**

Use your 3 cm by 3 cm piece of card. Draw a letter of the alphabet so that it fills the card. Here is an example:

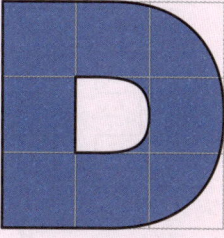

Cut out your letter and use it to create images which have no lines of symmetry, two lines of symmetry and four lines of symmetry. You might rotate or flip your letter.

# 14.7 Symmetrical pictures and diagrams

**1** Complete these shapes so that they have two lines of symmetry.

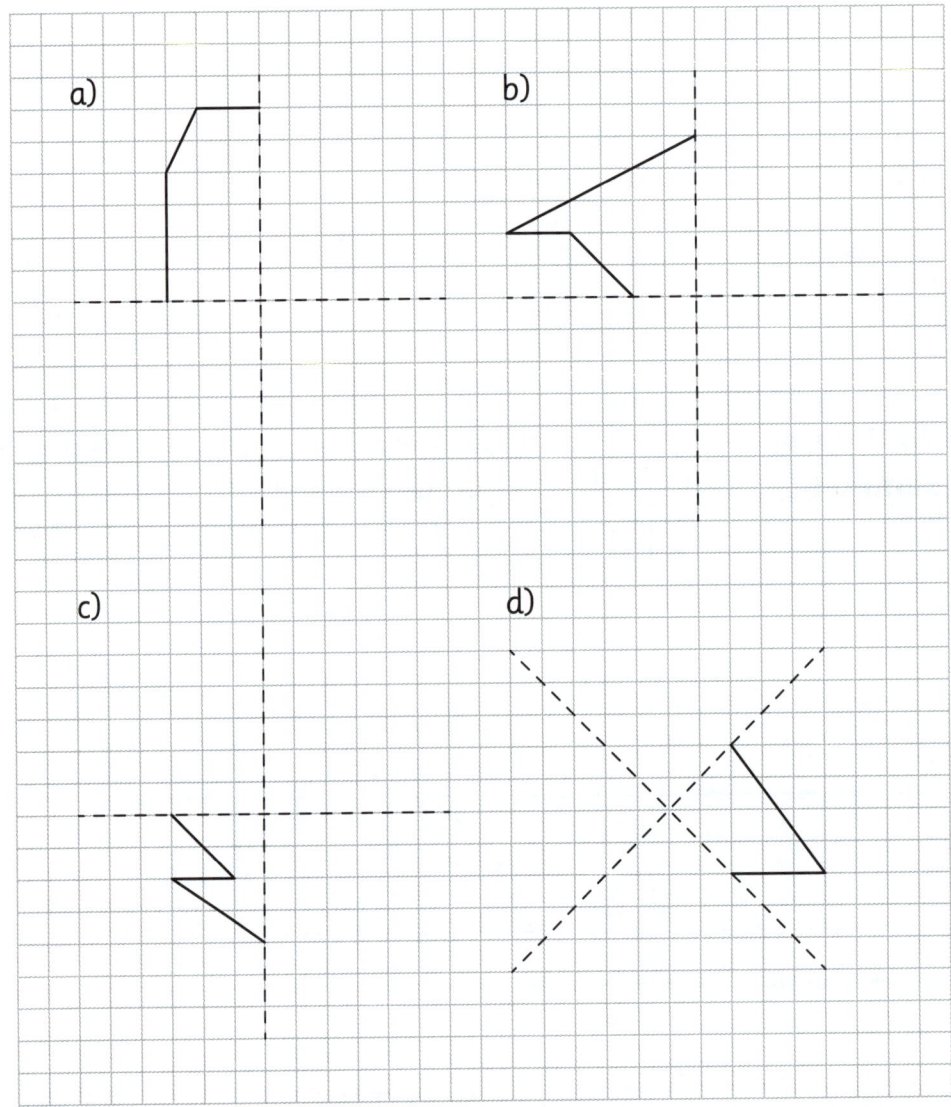

**2** You will need to use red, white and blue. Colour each flag in the correct colours. Underneath each flag write the number of lines of symmetry it has.

Scotland

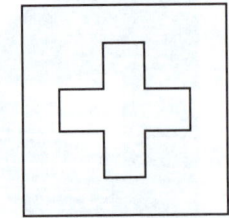

Switzerland

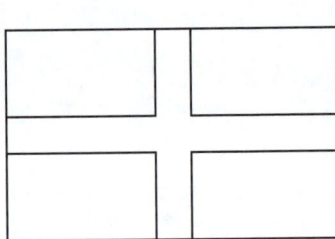

England

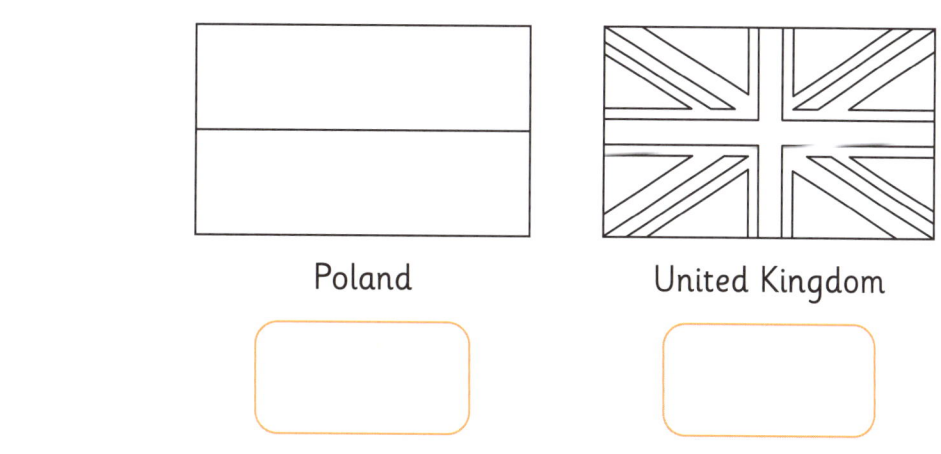

Poland

United Kingdom

**3** Decide if these statements are **always true**, **sometimes true** or **never true**. Circle the answer in the box.

| Triangles have only one line of symmetry.<br><br>always    sometimes    never | Squares have four lines of symmetry.<br><br>always    sometimes    never |
|---|---|
| A circle has only one line of symmetry<br><br>always    sometimes    never | Regular pentagons have six lines of symmetry.<br><br>always    sometimes    never |

The number of lines of symmetry and the number of sides in regular polygons is the same.

always    sometimes    never

 **Challenge**

Colour this pattern using five colours so that it has two lines of symmetry.

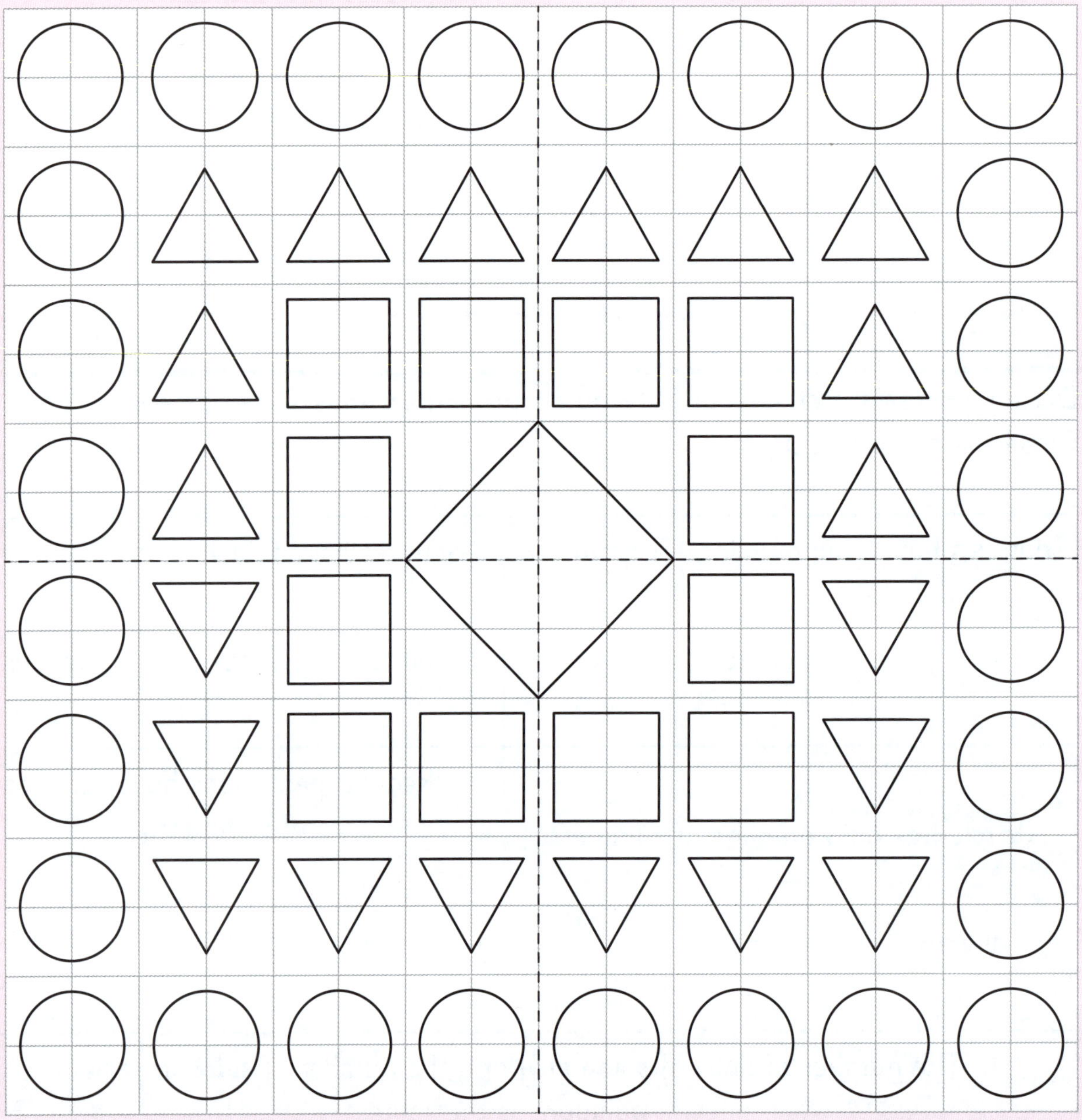

# 14.8 Reading scale maps

**1** Write down what each cm represents using these scales.

a)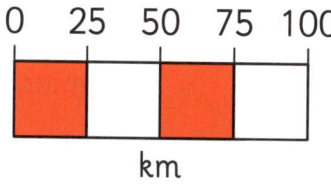

1 cm = 

b)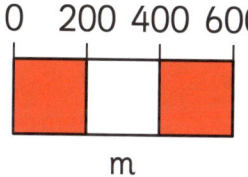

1 cm = 

c)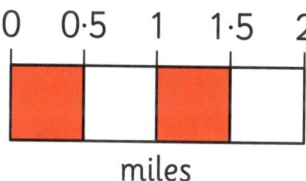

1 cm = 

d)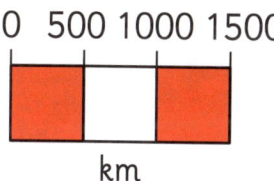

1 cm =

**2** Measure and complete these showing actual distance.

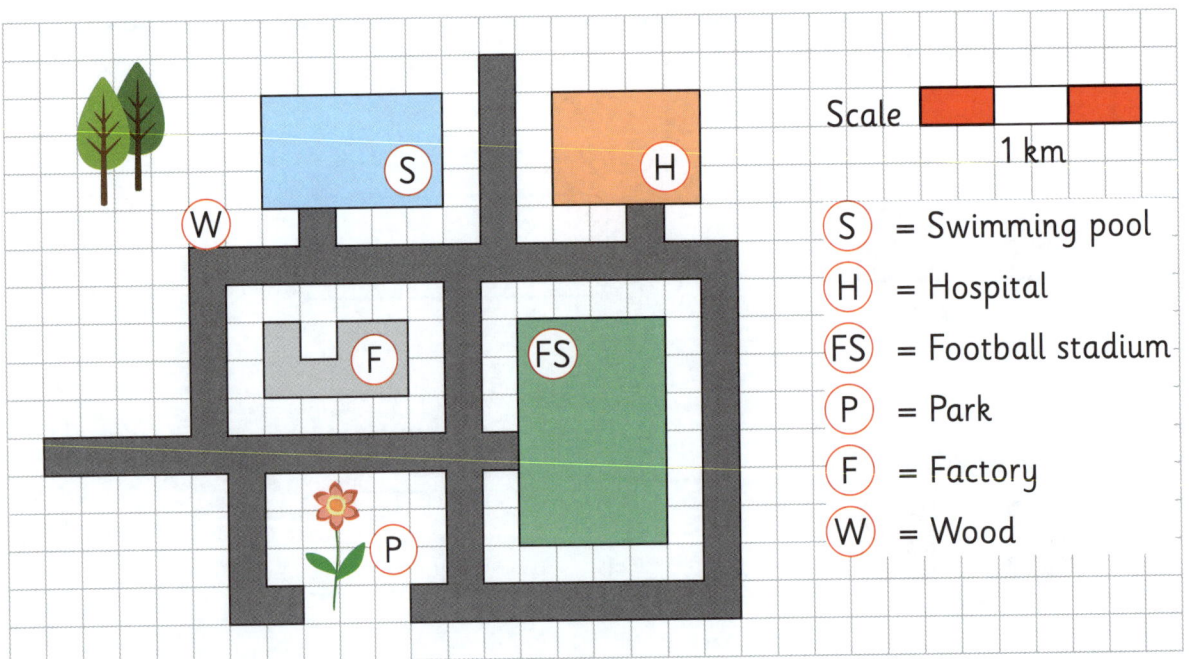

a) The entrance to the park is approximately ☐ km from the entrance to the woods.

b) The entrance to the hospital is approximately ☐ km from the entrance to the football stadium.

c) The entrance to the swimming pool is approximately ☐ km from the entrance to the woods.

d) The entrance to the swimming pool is approximately ☐ km from the entrance to the hospital.

e) The entrance to the hospital is approximately ☐ km from the entrance to the park.

f) The entrance to the ☐ is approximately 7 km from the entrance to the woods.

# Challenge

Use the space below to draw an animal park. Decide on your scale and mark it in.

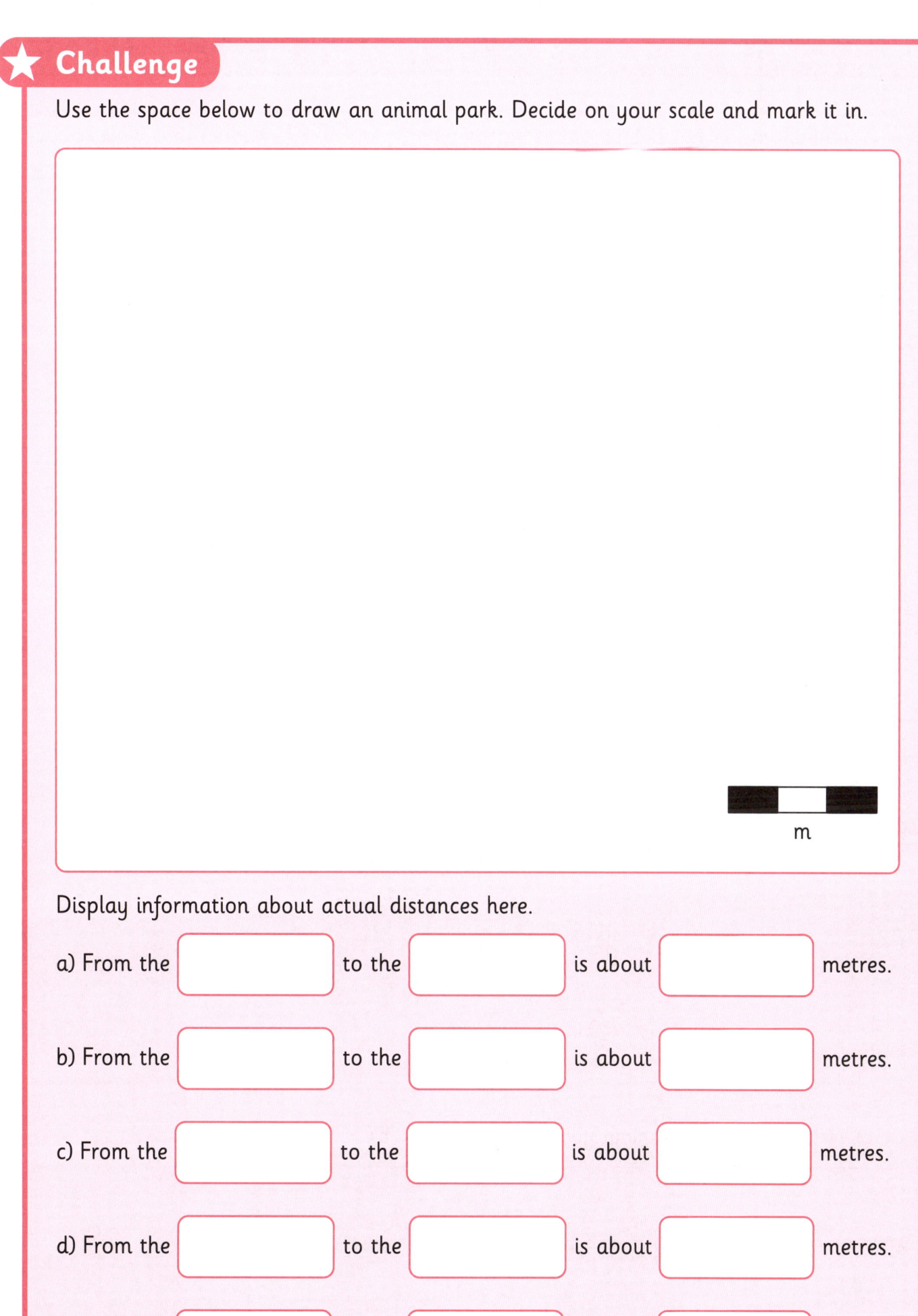

m

Display information about actual distances here.

a) From the ☐ to the ☐ is about ☐ metres.

b) From the ☐ to the ☐ is about ☐ metres.

c) From the ☐ to the ☐ is about ☐ metres.

d) From the ☐ to the ☐ is about ☐ metres.

e) From the ☐ to the ☐ is about ☐ metres.

# 15.1 Working with a range of graphs

1. The headteacher has been monitoring the number of P5–P7 children that walk to school in February and May. Her results are shown in the double bar graph below. Answer the questions that follow.

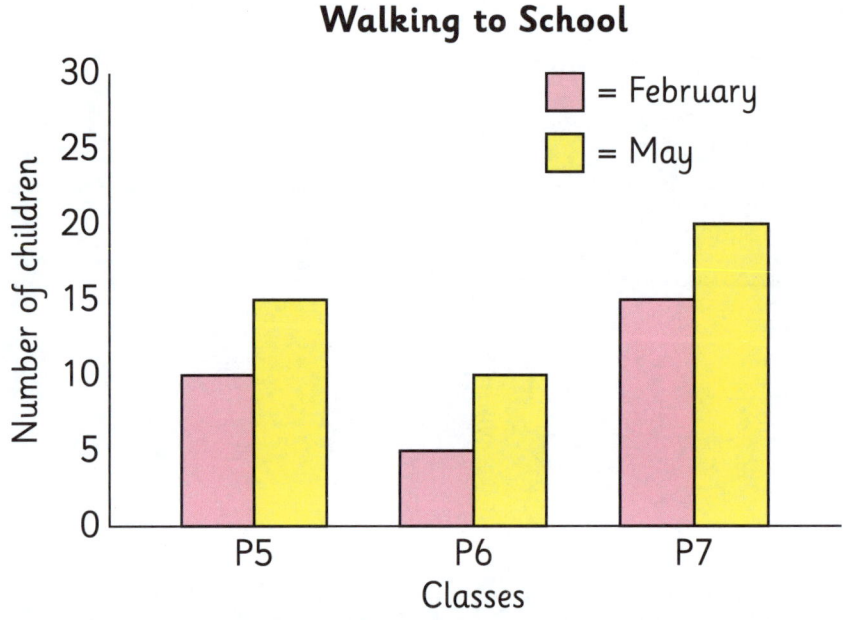

a) Which class shows most children walking to school in both February and May?

b) What do you notice when you compare the data for February and May?

c) Write a reason to explain your answer to part b)

2) Nuria and Isla have been selling badges to raise money. This double line graph shows how each girl got on. Answer the questions below the graph.

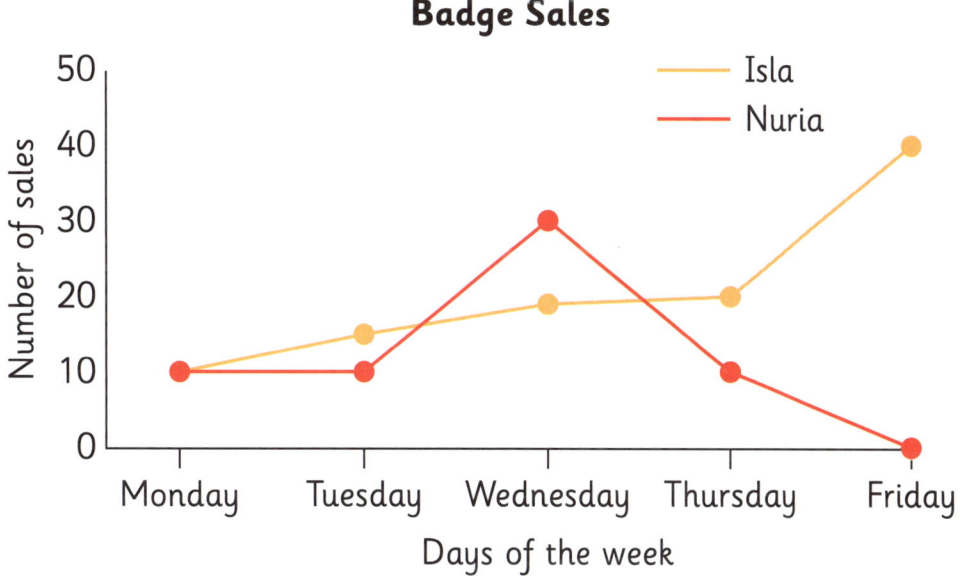

a) On Wednesday how many more badges did Nuria sell than Isla?

b) Who sold the most badges?

c) What reason might there be for Friday's sales?

## Challenge

Primary 6 and Primary 7 weighed the amount of food waste they had after lunch for a week. Their information is shown in the table. Look at this data and draw a double bar graph to display the information.

| Day | Primary 6 | Primary 7 |
|---|---|---|
| Monday | 950 grams | 800 grams |
| Tuesday | 900 grams | 700 grams |
| Wednesday | 900 grams | 750 grams |
| Thursday | 800 grams | 350 grams |
| Friday | 800 grams | 300 grams |

Write a question about this graph and ask a partner to answer it.

# 15.2 Using pie charts

**1** There are 24 children in Nuria's class. They are making a picnic. 12 of them chose cheese sandwiches, 6 of them chose ham sandwiches, 3 of them chose tuna sandwiches and 3 of them chose egg sandwiches. Colour and label this pie chart to show the information.

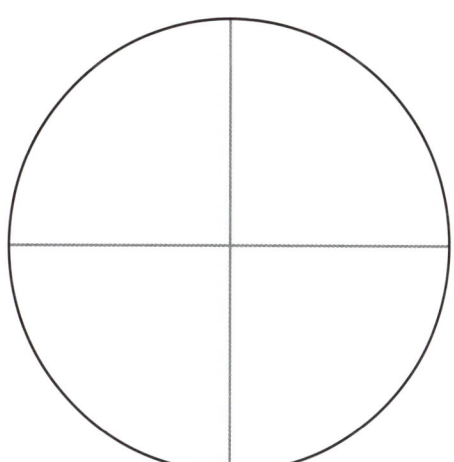

**2** There are 36 children in the school talent show.

18 of them sing.

9 of them dance.

5 of them tell jokes.

4 of them do magic tricks.

The pie chart has been divided into 36 sections. Each child is represented by  °.

Colour and label the pie chart to show the information.

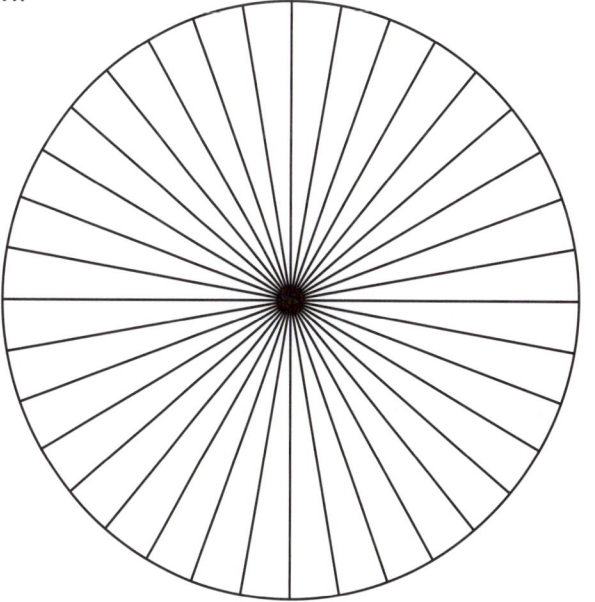

a) What do half of the children do?

b) What do one quarter of the children do?

c) One  of the children do magic tricks.

**3** 18 people were asked about the activities they did in their free time.

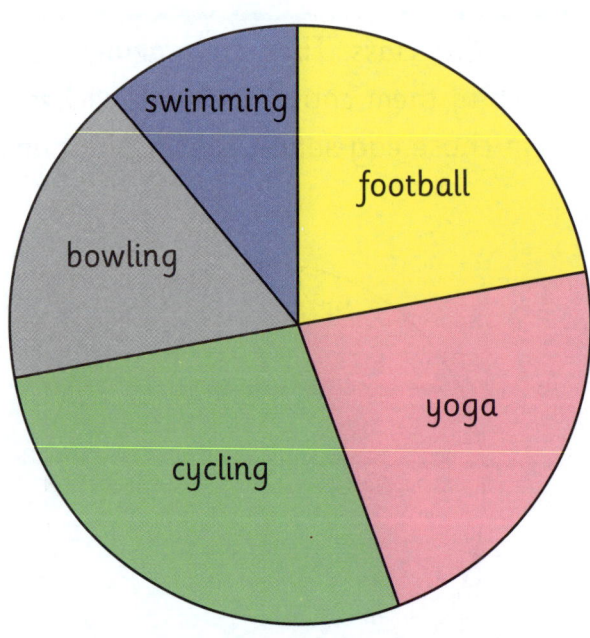

Measure each section to answer the questions. Hint: 360 ÷ 18 = 20°

a) Which is the most popular activity?

b) How many people go swimming?

c) How many more people go bowling than go swimming?

d) Which sports are equally popular?

## ★ Challenge

Finlay's mum goes shopping for gifts for her family. Look at the pie chart and answer the questions.

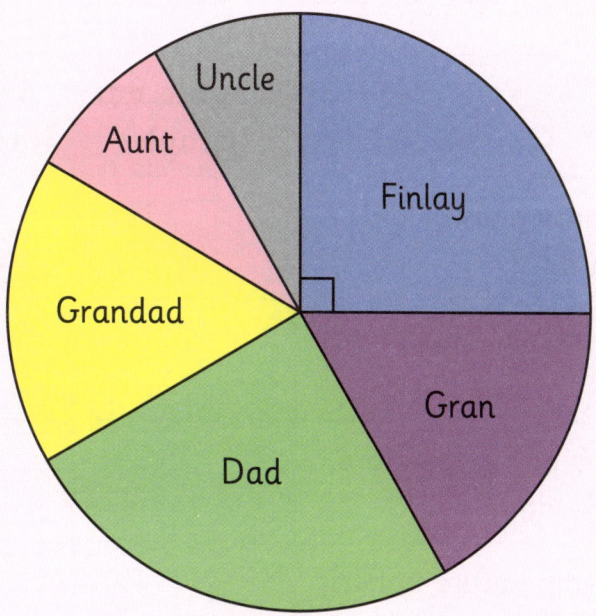

a) What fraction of the money did she spend on Finlay?

b) Finlay's mum spent **£40 on Gran**. Use this information to calculate how much she spent on everyone else.

Dad:

Grandad:

Aunt:

Uncle:

Finlay:

# 15.3 Creating and interpreting graphs

1. Decide which of these graphs would be best to display the data gathered from these questions. The first one is done for you.

| Question | Double bar graph | Double line graph | Pie chart |
|---|---|---|---|
| I wonder whether more boys or girls go to First Aid each day? | | | Yes |
| I wonder what subjects my classmates like best? | | | |
| I wonder whether P1 or P2 use more water throughout the day? | | | |
| I wonder how the temperature in Paris compares to Glasgow? | | | |
| I wonder which of the five new films is most popular at the cinema today? | | | |

2. Look at this pie chart. It shows the flowers used by Mrs Green, the florist, in April. Write true or false beside each statement.

**April Flowers**

(pie chart showing: orchids, tulips, daffodils, roses, lilies)

a) "I notice that orchids are the most popular flower."

b) "I notice that orchids and lilies make up half of all the flowers used."

c) "I notice that lilies are the least popular flower."

d) "I notice that the number of lilies and daffodils are about the same as the number of tulips."

3) Look at this line graph. Write down three "I notice..." statements about it.

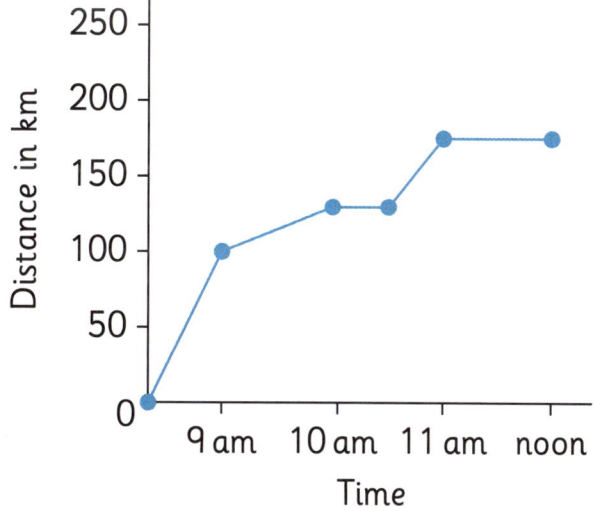

**Journey of a delivery driver**

"I notice ⎡                              ⎤"

"I notice ⎡                              ⎤"

"I notice ⎡                              ⎤"

## ⭐ Challenge

Write down two "I wonder…." questions that you could ask each of these groups.

a) The people you live with.

I wonder

I wonder

b) The people you are in class with.

I wonder

I wonder

c) The people you see on television or on film.

I wonder

I wonder

# 15.4 Drawing conclusions from graphs

1. a) Look at this bar graph. Decide if the statements are appropriate for the data shown. Circle yes or no.

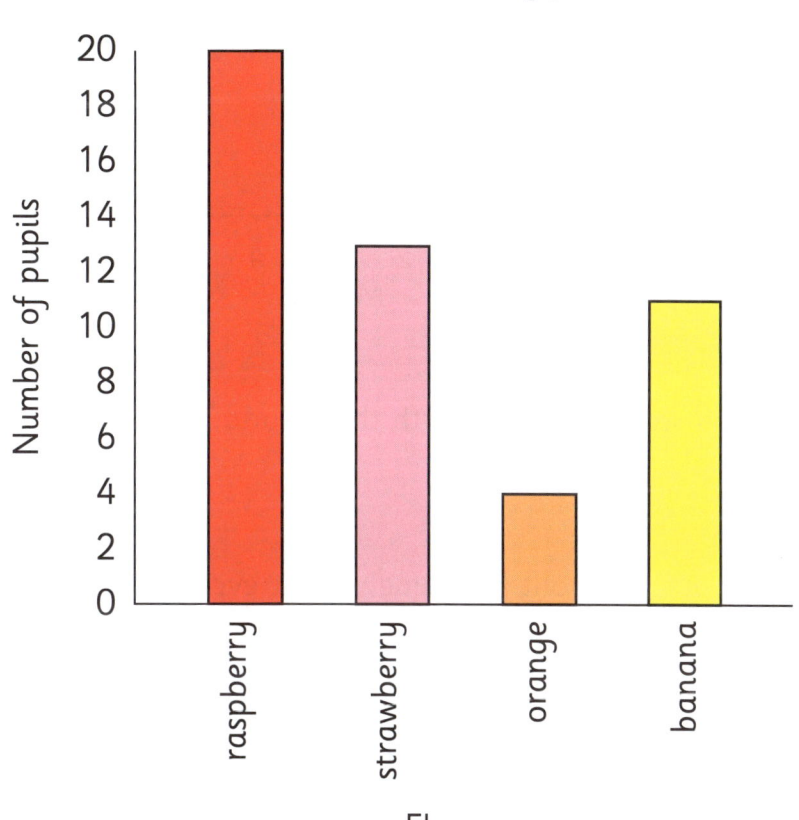

i) I found that red fruits are most popular.    YES    NO

ii) I wonder why banana lollies are so unpopular.    YES    NO

iii) I found that people would have liked to have lime as a choice.    YES    NO

iv) I think that the children who were asked were very young.    YES    NO

b) Now write an appropriate statement of your own about this graph.

**2** a) Look at this line graph. Decide if the statements are appropriate for the data shown. Write yes or no.

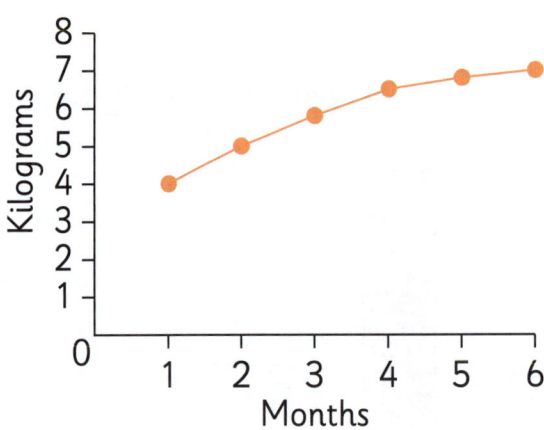

i) I wonder if Isla was heavier at birth than Nuria.

ii) I think babies put on about the same weight every month.

iii) I found that Nuria almost doubled in weight in six months.

iv) I wonder why Isla lost weight.

b) Write one appropriate statement and one inappropriate statement for this inquiry.

3) Look at this pie chart. It shows the patterns that people would like for their new sofa. Decide if the statements are appropriate for the data shown. Circle yes or no.

**Sofa Choices**

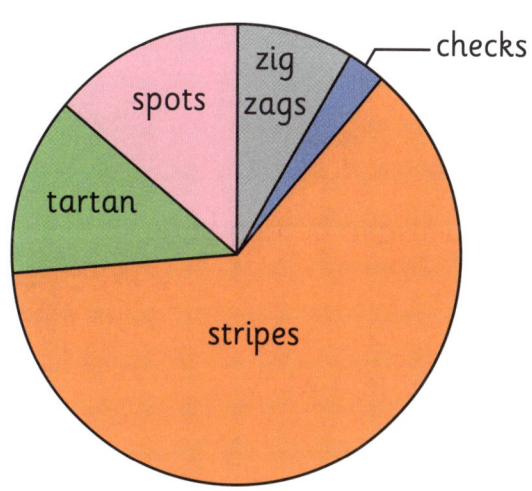

a) I found that more people would like stripes than any other pattern.   **YES   NO**

b) I wonder why checks and tartans have such similar results.   **YES   NO**

c) I found that less than 10 people like checks.   **YES   NO**

d) I think that the results would be different if people were allowed to choose no pattern.   **YES   NO**

## ★ Challenge

Think of five different questions that you are really interested in. You may not be able to carry out the investigation but your question should be able to be answered by data. An example is given:

- I wonder if more men or women go to my local gym before 9am each day?

# 16.1 Investigating the possible outcome of random events

**1** Write the words **certain**, **likely**, **even chance**, **unlikely** or **impossible** to describe the likelihood of these events occurring:

a) Tossing a coin and getting a tail

b) Mixing red and yellow paint and getting blue

c) Going to sleep at some point in a week

d) Meeting a prince

e) Growing a banana tree from an apple pip

f) Seeing a red car on the journey home from school

g) Sitting with a friend at lunch time

**2** Isla has a bag with 10 shapes in it.

Pick from the words **certain**, **likely**, **even chance**, **unlikely** or **impossible** to say how likely each of these is:

a) Isla pulls out a pentagon.

b) Isla pulls out a rectangle.

c) Isla pulls out a shape with more than three sides.

**3** Nuria has a six-sided spinner. Write the percentage chance – 0%, 25%, 50%, 75% and 100% – to say how likely these are:

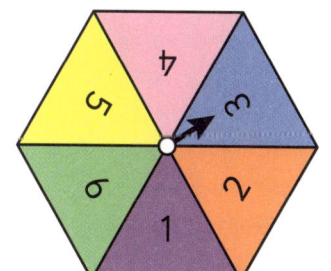

a) Nuria spins an even number.

b) Nuria spins a number less than 9.

**4** Write $0, \frac{1}{4}, \frac{1}{2}, \frac{3}{4}$, and 1 to show how likely these are:

a) Finlay picks an apple.

b) Finlay picks a yellow fruit.

## ★ Challenge

Colour the cubes so that the following are true. Your choices are red, purple, green, yellow, orange and blue.

- I have a 100% chance of drawing a colour with an **e** in the name.
- I have an even chance of drawing a colour with an **l** in the name.
- I have a 0·25 chance of drawing a colour with three vowels in the name.
- I have 0 chance of drawing a colour with a **d** in the name.

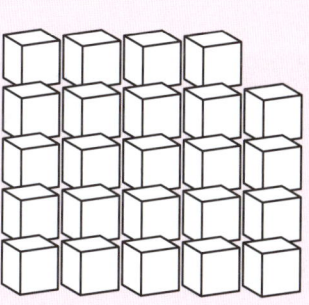